KU-538-528

Jelly Roll

Quilts

THE PERFECT GUIDE
TO MAKING THE
MOST OF THE LATEST
STRIP ROLLS

Jelly Roll Quilts

THE PERFECT GUIDE
TO MAKING THE
MOST OF THE LATEST
STRIP ROLLS

PAM & NICKY LINTOTT

David and Charles

A DAVID & CHARLES BOOK
Copyright © David & Charles Limited 2008

David & Charles is an F+W Publications Inc. company
4700 East Galbraith Road
Cincinnati, OH 45236

First published in the UK in 2008
First published in the US in 2008

Text and designs copyright © Pam Lintott and Nicky Lintott 2008
Photography and illustrations copyright © David and Charles 2008

Pam Lintott and Nicky Lintott have asserted their right to be
identified as authors of this work in accordance with the
Copyright, Designs and Patents Act, 1988.

All rights reserved. No part of this publication may be
reproduced, stored in a retrieval system, or transmitted, in any
form or by any means, electronic or mechanical, by photocopying,
recording or otherwise, without prior permission in writing from
the publisher.

The designs in this book are copyright and must not be stitched
for resale.

The author and publisher have made every effort to ensure
that all the instructions in the book are accurate and safe, and
therefore cannot accept liability for any resulting injury, damage
or loss to persons or property, however it may arise.

Names of manufacturers and products are provided for the
information of readers, with no intention to infringe copyright
or trademarks.

A catalogue record for this book is available from the British
Library.

ISBN-13: 978-0-7153-2863-7 paperback
ISBN-10: 0-7153-2863-8 paperback

Printed in China by SNP Leefung
for David & Charles
Brunel House, Newton Abbot, Devon

Commissioning Editor: Jane Trollope
Editorial Manager: Emily Pitcher
Assistant Editor: Sarah Wedlake
Project Editor: Cathy Joseph
Art Editor: Martin Smith
Designer: Eleanor Stafford
Production Controller: Kelly Smith
Photographers: Kim Sayer & Karl Adamson

Visit our website at www.davidandcharles.co.uk

David & Charles books are available from all good bookshops;
alternatively you can contact our Orderline on 0870 9908222 or
write to us at FREEPOST EX2 110, D&C Direct, Newton Abbot,
TQ12 4ZZ (no stamp required UK only); US customers call 800-
289-0963 and Canadian customers call 800-840-5220.

Contents

7 Introduction

8 Getting Started

9 Important Information

10 Bars of Gold

14 Blue Lagoon

20 Sparkling Gemstones

24 Garden Trellis

30 Nine Patch Wonder

36 Civil War Scrappy

40 Pandora's Box

46 Log Cabin Hidden Stars

54 Spiral Strips

62 Daisy Chain

70 Floral Bouquet

78 Friendship Braid

84 Pineapple Surprise

92 Twin Stars

100 Starlight Express

108 Both Sides of the Pond

116 Quilt Carry Bag

120 General Techniques

126 Acknowledgements

127 Useful Contacts

128 Index

Introduction

Have you purchased a gorgeous jelly roll of 40 2½in wide strips which looks so beautiful you don't like to unroll it? This book will encourage you to take those first steps. Go on, undo the ribbon and let it loose to reveal all those different fabrics. Just flick through these pages and see the quilts you can make with just one roll! Or perhaps you have fabric in your stash that is just waiting to be cut up into 2½in wide strips?

I founded The Quilt Room in 1981 and the shop in Dorking, England is a haven for quilters who come from far and wide. I now run it with my daughter Nicky and a team of loyal staff who between them have clocked up over 150 years working at The Quilt Room.

From the very beginning, teaching the art of patchwork and quilting has been a priority and over the years, not only has much work been generated from the workshops, but also much fun and laughter! In the same vein, our 'Strip Club' is held at The Quilt Room on the first Monday in every month.

Since Moda introduced its inspirational jelly rolls, we became obsessed with creating quilts using these 2½in wide strips. We started looking at quilt designs and working out just what could be produced with just one jelly roll.

Our enthusiasm became all-consuming and shop fabrics were ruthlessly cut up and made into 2½in wide strip bundles. Now we have strip bundles in virtually every basic range and colour way – it's a miracle there is still fabric left on the bolt!

People turn up eagerly to the Strip Club, awaiting a new quilt and new bundle of fabric. We like to be kept on our toes and are always trying to find new and inventive ways of using the strips.

Some of the quilts in this book have been introduced at Strip Club meetings and some are brand new. We hope you will enjoy trying them and that they will inspire you to create your own. Enjoy.

Getting started

What is a jelly roll? It is a roll of 40 fabrics cut in 2½in (6¼cm) wide strips across the width of the fabric (approximately 42in/105cm). Moda Fabrics introduced jelly rolls to showcase new fabric ranges. What a wonderful idea to have one 2½in wide strip of each new fabric wrapped up so deliciously! Our thanks go to Moda for inspiring us and allowing us to use the name jelly roll in our book.

If you want to make any of the quilts in this book and don't have a jelly roll to use, then cut a 2½in wide strip from 40 fabrics from your stash and you can follow all the instructions in just the same way.

If you prefer a less 'scrappy' quilt and wish to use fewer fabrics, then refer to the table on page 126 for fabric quantities. Most of the quilts in the book can be made using fat quarters but remember that the length of a strip cut from a fat quarter is half that of one cut from the full width, so you will need double the number of strips.

Important information

Measurements: Jelly rolls from Moda are cut 2½in (6¼cm) wide and at The Quilt Room we have continued to cut our strip bundles 2½in wide. When quilt making, it is impossible to mix metric and imperial measurements. It would be absurd to have a 2½in strip and tell you to cut it around 6cm to make a square! It wouldn't be square and nothing would fit.

This caused a dilemma when writing instructions for our quilts and a decision had to be made. All our instructions for using strips are therefore written in inches. Other fabric requirements, for borders, background fabric and binding, are given in both metric and imperial.

Washing note: It is important that pre-cut strips are not washed before use.

Seam allowance: We cannot stress enough the importance of maintaining an accurate scant ¼in seam allowance throughout. Please read through the General Techniques section on pages 120–125 and take the time to check your seam allowance with the test at the back of the book.

Quilt size: In this book we have shown what can be achieved with just one jelly roll. We have sometimes added background fabric and borders but the basis of each quilt is just one roll. If you want to make a larger version of any quilt, please refer to the instructions on page 124 to calculate your requirements.

Bars of Gold

Vital statistics

Quilt size: 69 x 66in.
Block size: 8 x 10in.
Number of blocks: 40 plus 3in wide sashing and border strips.

Sometimes you can just let the fabric talk for itself. The beautiful and distinctive fabrics designed by Kaffe Fassett come into that category. This quilt design is extremely quick and easy to complete but just look how the fabric works. If you have been worried about using fabrics with large designs and bright colours, perhaps it will encourage you to have a go.

This quilt has a number of names including *Stacked Coins* or *Chinese Coins*. However, using these rich and vibrant fabrics, we felt *Bars of Gold* was far more appropriate. We chose a deep mauve for the sashing and borders to set off the fabric.

What you need

• One jelly roll or 40 2½in strips cut the width of the fabric.

• 1.8m (71in) of sashing and border fabric.

• 60cm (23½in) of fabric for binding.

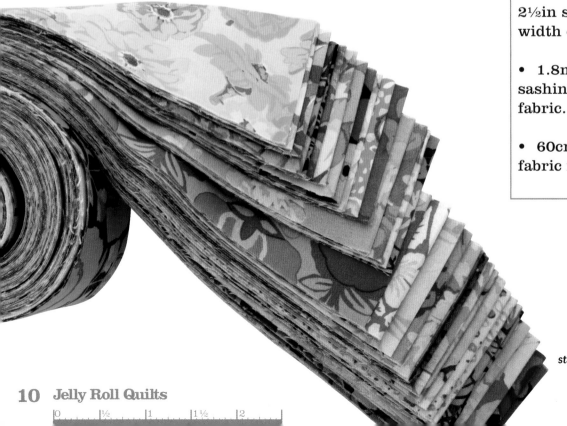

opposite:
A simple design allows the bright, bold fabrics of Kaffe Fassett to make their own statement. The quilt was pieced by the authors and longarm quilted by The Quilt Room.

Cutting instructions

Border and sashing: Cut nine 3½in wide strips the length of the border fabric.

Binding: Cut eight 2½in wide strips across the width of the binding fabric.

• Use a scant ¼in seam allowance throughout.

Sewing your strips

1. Sew five assorted strips together along their length. Repeat another seven times until all 40 strips are used (see diagram **a**).

2. Press the strip units and trim the selvedge. Cut the strip units into five 8in segments (see diagram **b**). You will have a total of 40 segments.

3. Now you can have fun deciding how to place your segments. Rotate some to make sure you don't have the same fabrics too near each other.

4. Lay out your quilt into six rows of six segments each (see diagram **c**). You will have four spare segments.

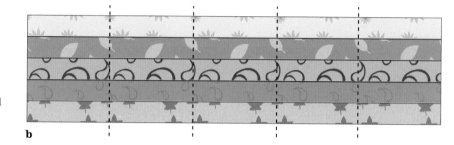

a

b

Sewing your quilt

Once you have decided where to place your segments, you are ready to sew your quilt. First sew the segments into vertical rows. Then measure them all. They should of course be all the same but you never know!

The length of the shortest one should be the length you cut your sashing strips and side borders. Your quilt will never be square if they are cut different lengths.

When attaching sashing and side borders to a vertical row, first pin the centre and ends of both the sashing and the vertical row together. You can then pin the rest, easing the strips if necessary. Sew all the sashing strips and side borders (see diagram **c**).

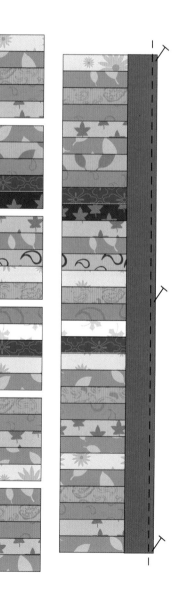

c

Tip

To prevent bowing in your strip units, it is best to sew two strips together and press before adding the third. Press before adding the fourth and press again before adding the fifth. Press all the seams in the same direction. Chain sew the strips whenever you can for speed.

0   ½   1   1½   2

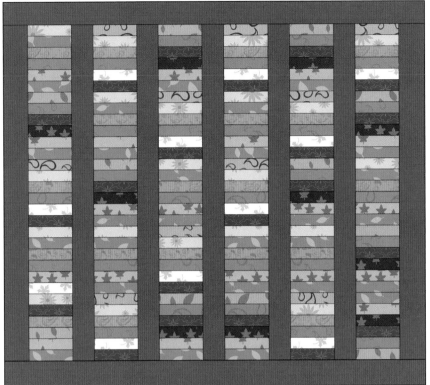

Sewing the top and bottom borders

Determine the horizontal measurement from side to side across the centre of the quilt top, as shown in diagram **d**. Cut a top and bottom border to this measurement and sew to the quilt. Your quilt top is now complete. Quilt as desired and bind to finish.

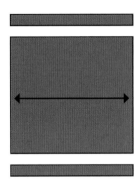

d

Tip

When it is necessary to ease fabric to fit, place the fabric that is longer on the bottom as the feed dogs will help with easing.

Blue Lagoon

This was the first quilt we introduced at our 'Strip Club' meetings at The Quilt Room and has been one of the most popular. We used one jelly roll combined with a white-on-white fabric for a gorgeous, fresh-looking quilt. We chose some light and dark strips for contrast in the four patch blocks but, apart from that, it required very little sorting of strips.

Blue Lagoon is an ideal quilt to make with a jelly roll as the quilt will look great whatever strips you put together. The variation, on page 17, shows just how stunning it looks made in fabrics inspired by the 1930s.

Vital statistics

Quilt size: 68 x 74in.
Block size: 4in.
Number of blocks: 110.
Setting: 10 x 11 blocks with 2in wide sashing and 3in wide border.

What you need

• One jelly roll or 40 2½in strips cut the width of the fabric, to include 14 each of light and dark (or contrasting) fabrics and nine assorted (you will have three spare).

• 2.5m (98½in) of background fabric for rectangles and borders.

• 60cm (23½in) of fabric for binding.

opposite:
Contrasting light and dark fabrics in the four patch blocks produces a fresh-looking design. The quilt was pieced by the authors and longarm quilted by The Quilt Room.

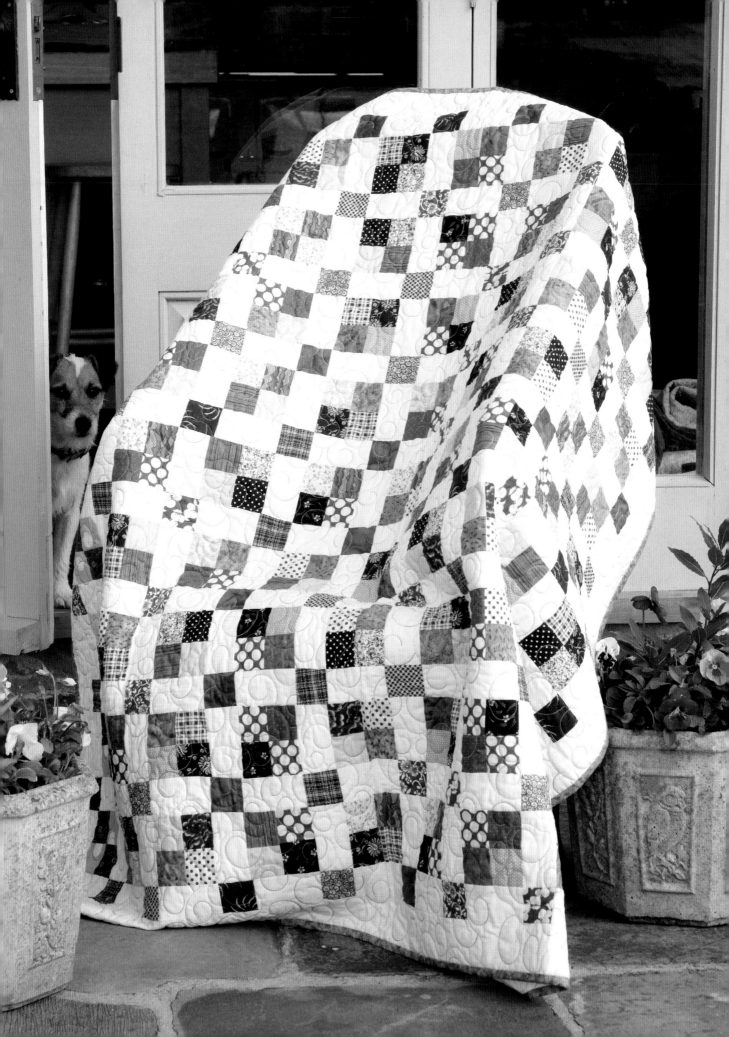

Cutting instructions

Nine assorted strips: Sub-cut these strips into 2½in squares. You should get 16 from each strip. You need 132.

Background fabric: From the background fabric, cut 27 2½in strips across the width of the fabric. Sub-cut these into 2½ x 4½in rectangles. You should get nine from each width of fabric. You need 241.

Borders: From the background fabric, cut eight 3½in wide strips across the width of the fabric.

Binding: Cut eight 2½in strips across the width of fabric.

● Use a scant ¼in seam allowance throughout.

Sewing the four patch blocks

1. Take one light strip and one dark strip from the jelly roll and lay right sides together. Sew down the long side. Open and press the seam to dark side (see diagram **a**).

2. Once you are confident the seam allowance is correct, join the remaining 13 light and 13 dark strips, chain piecing for speed (see page 122 for the technique). Open them out and press seams to the dark side as shown. You will now have 14 strip units. From each strip unit sub-cut 16 2½in wide segments (see diagram **b**).

a

b

3. Chain piece the 2½in wide segments together to form the four patch blocks. Cut threads and press the four patch blocks open (see diagram **c**). The centre seams will nest together nicely as they are all pressed to the dark side, but if necessary use a pin to ensure a perfect match. You need 110 four patch blocks.

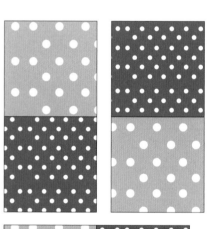

c

Tip

After step 1, above, check your seam allowance. Remember that it should be an accurate, scant ¼in. If the joined strips do not measure 4½in across then you must adjust your seam allowance.

|0 |½ |1 |1½ |2 |

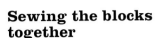

Sewing the blocks together

1. Create the first row by sewing a 2½in square, cut from the nine assorted strips, to the left-hand side of 10 rectangles, cut from the background fabric, and a 2½in square to the right-hand side of the last rectangle (see diagram **d**). Make 12 of these rows.

2. Create the second row by sewing a 2½in x 4½in rectangle to the left-hand side of 10 four patch blocks and a rectangle to the right-hand side of the last block (see diagram **e**). Make 11 of these rows.

Tip

When cutting the 2½in segments to form your four patch blocks, you can layer one strip unit right sides together with another, reversing light and dark. The seams will nest together nicely. When you sub-cut your 2½in wide segments, they will then be ready to sew together to make your four patch blocks.

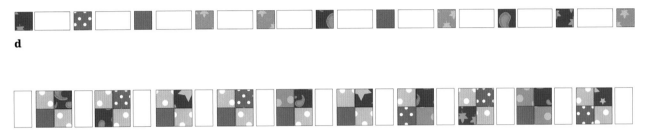

d

e

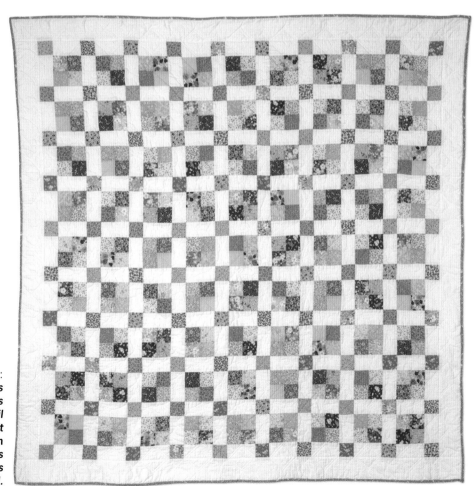

right:
Variation entitled Fresh in fabrics inspired by the 1930s. The quilt was pieced and quilted by Gail Parker. Gail attended the first meeting of The Quilt Room 'Strip Club' when the Blue Lagoon pattern was introduced. This quilt is smaller than given in the instructions as only 30 strips were used.

f

Sewing the rows

Referring to diagram **f,** above, sew the rows together, alternating the strips. Pin at every seam intersection before sewing to ensure the perfect match. **Note**: The finished quilt (right) is smaller as only 30 strips were used.

Finishing the quilt

Join your eight 3½in wide border strips into one continuous length and, referring to the instructions on page 122, add borders to the quilt. Your quilt top is now complete. Quilt as desired and bind to finish.

0   ½   1   1½   2

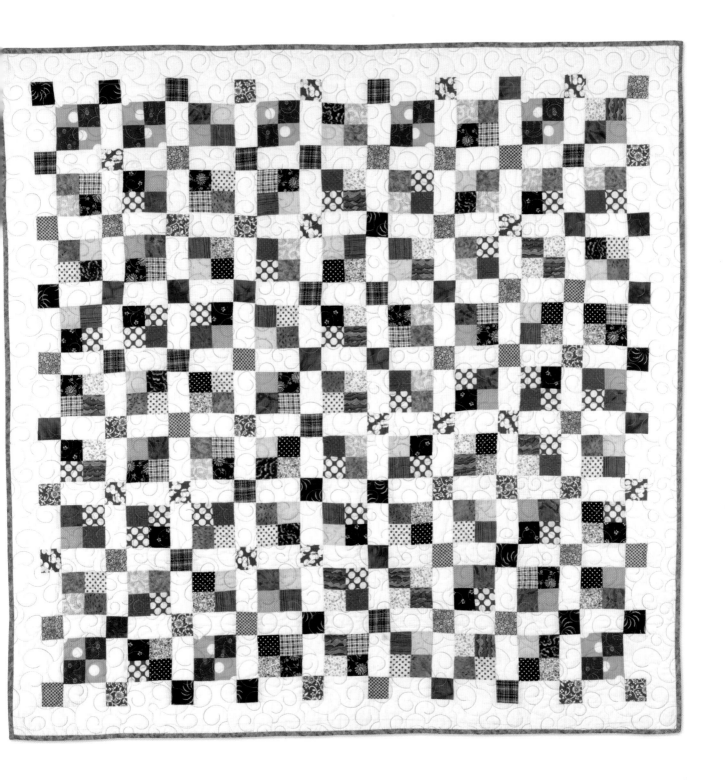

Sparkling Gemstones

Vital statistics

Quilt size: 58 x 76in.
Block size: 6in.
Number of blocks: 108
Setting: 9 x 12 blocks plus 2in wide border.

Like the first quilt, *Bars of Gold*, this also uses Kaffe Fassett's vivid fabrics and, again, is quick and easy to put together. In this instance we have used a light stone-coloured background to make our 'gems' stand out and sparkle even more.

This is a great quilt for using large-scale prints and you could easily choose some novelty fabrics for a bright, fun 'first bed' quilt.

What you need

• One jelly roll or 40 assorted 2½in strips, cut the width of the fabric.

• 1.6m (63in) of background fabric.

• 50cm (20in) of fabric for the border.

• 50cm (20in) of fabric for the binding.

opposite:
The gorgeous, bright colours of Kaffe Fassett's fabrics contrast with a pale background. The quilt was pieced by the authors and longarm quilted by The Quilt Room.

Cutting instructions

Background: Cut 40 1½in wide strips across the width of fabric.

Border: Cut seven 2½in strips across the width of fabric.

Binding: Cut seven 2½in strips across the width of fabric.

● Use a scant ¼in seam allowance throughout.

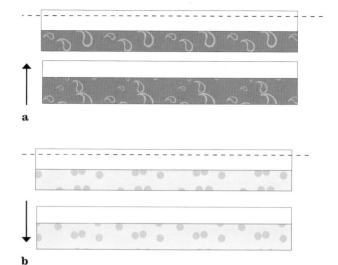

a

b

Sewing the blocks

1. Take one 2½in strip from the jelly roll and one 1½in background strip and, with right sides together, sew together down the long side. Press the seam open towards the background strip (see arrow in diagram **a**).

2. Take another strip from the jelly roll and one background strip and sew together, as before, down the long side. Press the seam open towards the jelly roll strip (see arrow in diagram **b**).

3. Take these two strip units and sew, with right sides together, down the length of the jelly roll strips (see diagram **c**).

4. Press open, making sure that the centre seam is pressed in the same direction as the two other seams (see arrows in diagram **d**).

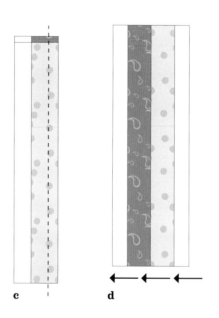

c   **d**   **e**

5. Cut 3½in segments from the strip unit, as indicated in diagram **e**. You will get 11 segments. Keep in one pile. Repeat with the other jelly roll strips and background strips. You will have 20 separate piles of 11 segments each, making a total of 220 segments. Four of these are spare.

6. Choose two different segments and sew them right sides together, making sure that you rotate one segment so that the seams are going in the opposite direction (see diagram **f**). They will then nest together to ensure there is a perfect match.

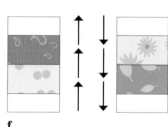

f

7. Make 108 blocks, aiming for four different fabrics in each block (see diagram **g**).

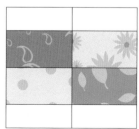

g

Assembling your blocks

Referring to diagram **h**, lay out the blocks into rows, rotating every other block 90 degrees. Make 12 rows of nine blocks. When you are happy with the layout, sew blocks into rows and then sew rows together.

Finishing the quilt

Join your seven 2½in border strips into one continuous length and, referring to the instructions on page 122, add the borders to your quilt. Your quilt top is now complete. Quilt as desired and bind to finish.

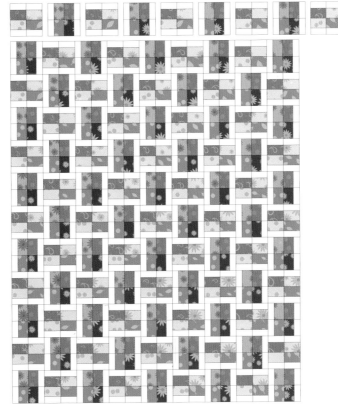

h

Tip

Keep your patchwork neat and tidy by always snipping threads as you go. It will make a big difference to your work and is a very good habit to get into.

Garden Trellis

Vital statistics

Quilt size: 56 x 67in.
Block size: 11in.
Number of blocks: 20.
Setting: 4 x 5 blocks plus 6in wide border.

For this garden-inspired quilt we used a pretty country range from Blackbird Designs. Their assortment of colours is always pleasing to the eye and this range contains a mixture of reds, creams, greens and blues. This quilt goes together very quickly and, although you have to handle the bias edges with a little respect, it is a quick and easy choice if you need a speedy present for a special friend.

Our variation entitled *It's Not a Gold Watch!*, on page 27, is a much larger version made in aqua and cream – a sophisticated combination that worked very well.

What you need

• One jelly roll or 40 2½in wide strips cut the width of the fabric (half light and half dark).

• 1.1m (43in) fabric for borders.

• 50cm (20in) fabric for binding.

opposite:
Garden Trellis *uses a soothing mix of country colours from Blackbird Designs. The quilt was pieced by the authors and longarm quilted by The Quilt Room.*

Cutting instructions

Border: Cut six 6½in wide strips across the width of the fabric.

Binding: Cut seven 2½in wide strips across the width of the fabric.

• Use a scant ¼in seam allowance throughout.

Tip

The Omnigrid 98L (see Tools on page 120) makes cutting this quilt very easy but if you don't have one of these triangles a rotary cutting square may be used instead.

Sewing the strips

1. Take one light and one dark strip and sew together to form a strip unit as shown in diagram **a**. Press the seam towards the dark side as indicated. Repeat until all strips are used.

a

2. Take two strip units and place right sides together, reversing the lights and the darks. Make sure the centre seams nest up against each other all the way along the strip unit. Pin in place to stop any movement. Sew a scant ¼in seam along both sides of the strip unit to form a tube (see diagram **b**). You will have 10 tubes.

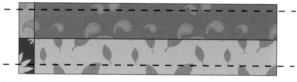

b

Cutting the strip units

1. You are now going to cut the tubes into triangles using the Omnigrid 98L. Lay the triangle on the tube. Line up the 3½in line along the centre seam and the 7½in line along the bottom seam. The marked top of the triangle will touch the top seam. Always make sure to line up your centre seam to make sure you are not going askew.

2. Cut either side of the triangle, then position the triangle along the tube. When you cut the second triangle you create another two triangles. You will get eight triangles from the tube (see diagram **c**).

3. Gently pick up each triangle and unpick the few threads that are along the tip of the triangle (see diagram **d**). You are dealing with bias edges now so great care must be taken not to pull the fabric too much.

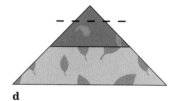

d

4. Gently press open, pressing seams towards the darker side. This is a quarter block (see diagram **e**). Repeat with all your tubes. You need 80 quarter blocks.

e

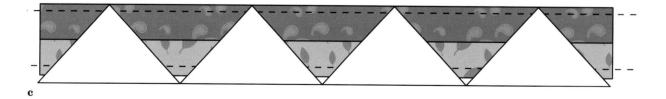

c

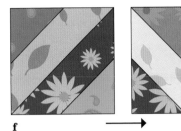

f

g

Assembling your blocks

1. Lay all your quarter blocks out, making sure a dark triangle is top left on one block and a light triangle is top right on the other (see diagram **f**). This will ensure darks and lights are reversed. When you are happy with the overall effect, sew two quarter blocks together to form half blocks, matching seams. Repeat with all your quarter blocks. Press to the dark centre triangle as shown by the arrow.

2. Sew two half blocks together as shown in diagram **g**, making sure you have lights next to darks and matching seams. Press seams gently. You will have 20 blocks.

Left:

This variation of Garden Trellis, entitled It's Not a Gold Watch! was made by the authors for Hilary, who manages The Quilt Room mail order department. Coming up to 25 years of service, there were lots of hints as to the colour of her bedroom – so they obliged and used a range of aqua and cream!

Tip

If you don't have an Omnigrid 98L and are using a rotary cutting square, position it with the 0 at the top and place a piece of tape from the left 6½in marking to the right 6½in marking. This is your guide to place along the bottom edge of your tube.

h

Sewing your blocks together

Referring to diagram **h**, above, sew the blocks together to form rows and then sew the rows together.

Finishing the quilt

Join your six 6½in border strips into one continuous length and, referring to the instructions on page 122, add the borders to your quilt. Your quilt top is now complete. Quilt as desired and bind to finish.

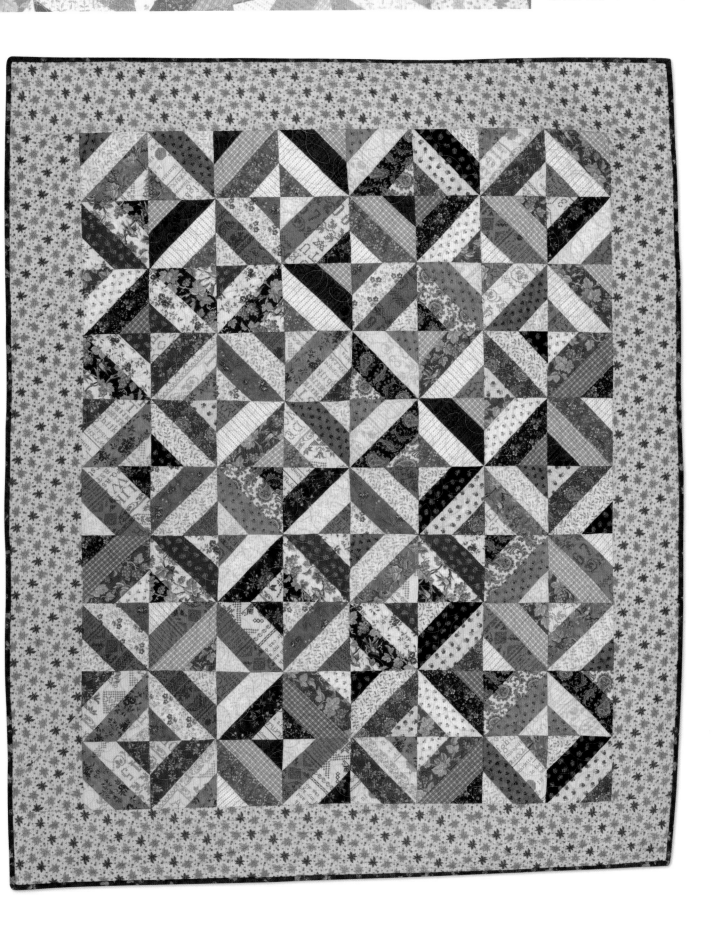

Nine Patch Wonder

Vital statistics

Quilt size: 64 x 76in.
Block size: 6in.
Number of blocks: 120.
Setting: 10 x 12 blocks plus 2in wide border.

What you need

• **One jelly roll or 40 2½in wide strips cut the width of the fabric from an antique reproduction range.**

• 1.2m (47in) first fabric (A) for hourglass blocks.

• 1.2m (47in) second fabric (B) for hourglass blocks.

• 50cms (20in) border fabric.

• 60cms (24in) binding fabric.

If there were a poll for the favourite and most versatile block of all time, our guess is that the nine patch would be up around the top. There is so much you can do with it – the possibilities are endless.

Now the interesting fact is that you can make 60 nine patch blocks from one jelly roll. With that in mind, you could start sewing nine patches and make different quilts for every day of the week.

You could piece them together with sashing strips, you could alternate them with plain blocks or you could choose to set them on point for a totally different look.

We have chosen just two options to show you in the next two quilts. In the first, we have alternated the nine patch block with an hourglass block and used the subtle colours from Lecien's Antique range. Look out for the second option in the *Civil War Scrappy* quilt on page 36.

opposite:
The hourglass block is in gentle pink and grey blue, which lends itself perfectly to a soft, antique looking quilt. The quilt was pieced by the authors and longarm quilted by The Quilt Room.

Cutting instructions

Hourglass blocks: With fabric A, cut six strips 7¼in wide across the width of the fabric. Sub-cut into five 7¼in squares.

With fabric B, cut six strips 7¼in wide across the width of the fabric. Sub-cut into five 7¼in squares.

Border: Cut seven 2½in wide strips across the width of the fabric.

Binding: Cut eight 2½in wide strips across the width of the fabric.

• Use a scant ¼in seam allowance throughout.

Sewing the nine patch blocks

1. Pair up the 40 antique reproduction print strips. Take one pair of strips and cut each into three lengths of 14in (see diagram **a**).

2. From your six lengths, assemble two strip segments. Press seams to the darker side (see diagram **b**).

3. Cut each into five 2½in wide segments. (see diagram **c**).

4. Make three nine patch blocks (see diagram **d**). You will have one segment spare. Repeat with the other pairs of strips. You need 60 nine patch blocks altogether, which will use the whole of the jelly roll.

a

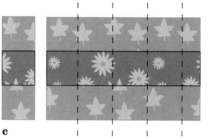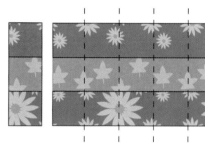

b

c

d

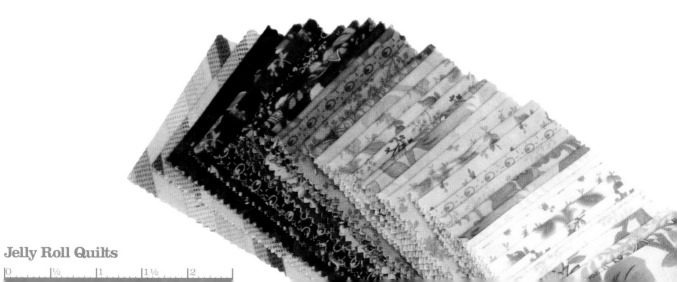

|0 |½ |1 |1½ |2

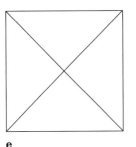

e

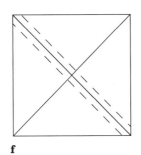

f

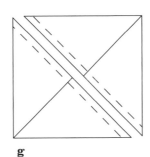

g

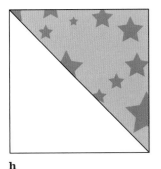

h

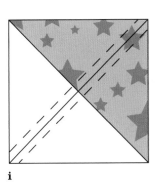

i

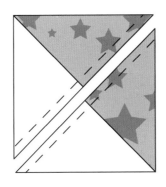

j

Quick piecing the hourglass blocks

1. Take one of your fabric A 7¼in squares and, on the wrong side, draw diagonal lines from corner to corner in both directions (see diagram **e**).

2. With right sides together, lay the marked fabric A square on top of a fabric B square. Sew a ¼in seam allowance on both sides of one diagonal line (see diagram **f**). Press the stitching to set, without opening. Cut the units apart between stitching, cutting on the drawn line (see diagram **g**).

3. Open the units and press seam to darker side (see diagram **h**).

4. On the wrong side of one unit, continue the drawn line into the other corner. Lay this unit on top of the other unit, right sides together, making sure you have opposite fabrics facing. Sew a ¼in seam allowance on both sides of the diagonal line. Press stitching to set seam. Cut units apart between stitching as before (see diagram **i**).

5. Press open to reveal two hourglass blocks (see diagram **j**). Repeat until you have 60 hourglass blocks.

Tip

When displaying quilts, it is very important that the weight of the quilt is evenly distributed. Use this method for making a sleeve to hold a pole or batten and the quilt will hang well: Cut a 6-8in (15–20cm) strip of fabric the width of your quilt. Hem the raw edges on the short sides. Stitch the long sides together and turn right side out to form a tube or sleeve. Position the sleeve at the back of the quilt with the top edge of the sleeve just below the edge of the quilt binding. Sew by hand to the back of the quilt along the top and bottom of the sleeve. Insert a pole or batten and hang from supports at each end.

k

Sewing your blocks together

Referring to diagram **k**, join the blocks
together, alternating the nine patch
blocks with the hourglass blocks. Pin
all intersecting seams before sewing to
ensure a perfect match.

Finishing the quilt

Join your seven 2½in wide border
strips into one continuous length
and, referring to the instructions
on page 122, add borders to
the quilt. Your quilt top is now
complete. Quilt as desired and
bind to finish.

|0   ½ |1   1½   2

Civil War Scrappy

Vital statistics

Quilt size: 60 x 84in.
Block size: 6in.
Number of blocks: 117.
Setting: 9 x 13 blocks plus 3in wide border.

For our second quilt using the nine patch block, we have chosen to alternate it with a snowball block and have used reproduction fabrics from the American Civil War era to create a dynamic effect. The snowball blocks give plenty of space to show off your quilting talents. Let your imagination take over – both this quilt and the previous *Nine Patch Wonder* could look just as impressive in totally different fabrics.

What you need

- One jelly roll or 40 2½in wide reproduction print strips cut the width of fabric.

- 1.8m (71in) of background fabric for snowball blocks.

- 1m (39in) fabric for snowball block corners.

- 70cm (27½in) border fabric.

- 60cm (23½in) binding fabric.

opposite:
Our Civil War strip roll combined a mixture of fabrics from designers Judie Rothermel of Marcus Brothers and Jo Morton of Andover Fabrics. They blend together beautifully to create an authentic looking quilt, which was pieced by the authors and longarm quilted by The Quilt Room.

Cutting instructions

Snowball blocks: From the background fabric, cut ten 6½in wide strips across the width of the fabric. Sub-cut into 6½in squares. You need 58.

Corners for snowball blocks: Cut 15 2½in wide strips across the width of the fabric. Sub-cut into 2½in squares. You will need 232.

Border: Cut seven 3½in wide strips across the width of the fabric.

Binding: Cut eight 2½in wide strips across the width of the fabric.

● Use a scant ¼in seam allowance throughout.

Making the snowball blocks

1. Draw a diagonal line from corner to corner on the wrong side of the snowball block corner 2½in squares (see diagram **a**).

2. With right sides together, lay a marked square on one corner of a 6½in background square, aligning the outer edges. Sew across the diagonal, using the marked diagonal line as the stitching line (see diagram **b**). After a while you may find you do not need to draw the line as it is not difficult to judge the sewing line. Repeat on the other three corners.

3. Open the square out and press towards the outside of the block, aligning the raw edges. Fold the corner back down and trim the excess fabric ¼in beyond the stitching line. Repeat with all the corners to make 58 snowball blocks (see diagram **c**).

Making the nine patch blocks

1. Pair up the 40 strips from your jelly roll. Take one pair of strips and cut each into three lengths of 14in (see diagram **d**).

2. From your six lengths, assemble two strip segments. Press seams to darker side, as shown by arrows (see diagram **e**).

3. Cut each into five 2½in segments (see diagram **f**).

4. Make three nine patch blocks (see diagram **g**). You will have one segment spare. Repeat with the other pairs of strips until you have 59 nine patch blocks.

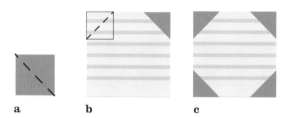

a b c

d

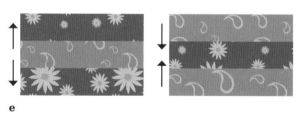

e

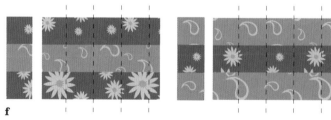

f

g

h

Sewing your blocks together

Referring to diagram **h**, join the blocks together, alternating the snowball blocks with the nine patch blocks. Pin the point where the snowball triangle joins the nine patch block before sewing to ensure a perfect match.

Finishing the quilt

Join your seven 3½in wide border strips into one continuous length and, referring to the instructions on page 122, add borders to the quilt. Your quilt top is now complete. Quilt as desired and bind to finish.

Pandora's Box

Vital statistics

Quilt size: 52 x 76in.
Block size: 8in.
Number of blocks: 40
Setting: 5 x 8 blocks plus 6in wide border.

The muted, earthy colours of Japanese taupes are subtle and sophisticated and blend together so well. This quilt would particularly complement a room that features natural materials, such as wood and leather.

We chose a black print border and quilted dragonflies all over, which added depth and texture. Our variation, shown on page 43, uses fabrics inspired by the 1930s and demonstrates just how different the quilt can look in other colourways.

What you need

• One jelly roll or 40 taupe 2½in strips, cut across the width of the fabric.

• 1.10m (43in) of fabric for borders.

• 50cm (20in) of fabric for binding.

opposite:
Pandora's Box uses Japanese taupes and looks stunning in a symmetrical design. The quilt was pieced by the authors and longarm quilted by The Quilt Room.

Cutting instructions

Taupe strips: Trim the selvedge and cut each strip into four rectangles: two of 2½ x 4½in and two of 2½ x 8½in. The remaining 18in or so of each strip is for making your four patch blocks.

Borders: Cut six 6½in wide strips across the width of the fabric.

Binding: Cut seven 2½in wide strips across the width of the fabric.

• Use a scant ¼in seam allowance throughout.

Making the four patch blocks

1. Using the strips you have saved for your four patch blocks, sew two contrasting strips together. Press seams to the dark side (see diagram **a**). Repeat until you have 20.

2. Cut each one of these joined strips into 2½in segments (see diagram **b**). You only need four from each joined strip for your quilt. Any extras can be used for a later project.

3. Rotate one segment and, matching the centre seams, sew your four patch, as shown in diagram **c**. You need 40. Press these open with the seams to the dark side.

Tip

Stack your cut pieces of taupe strips into four separate piles keeping the fabric in the same order, so that each pile is identical. This is very important if you want to chain piece.

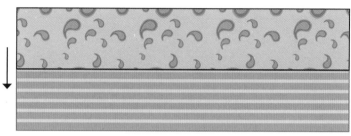

a

 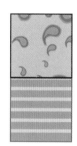  

b

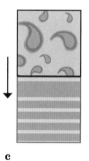 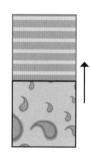 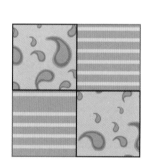

c

Tip

For accuracy, don't stackpile your strips when cutting the segments in diagram **b**. Check you are cutting perfect rectangles by putting one of your ruler guides on the seam line.

Constructing your blocks

1. Place your four separate piles of strips, which are in the same order, neatly to the side of your machine next to the pile of four patches.

2. Take a four patch block and sew a 4½in strip of the same fabric to either side of it. Press the seams away from the four patch (see diagram **d**).

3. Sew an 8½in strip of the same fabric to the top and bottom of this unit (see diagram **e**). You can chain piece these very quickly so long as you have your piles of fabric in the same order. Make 40 blocks. Press the seams away from the four patch, as shown.

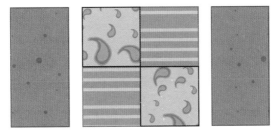

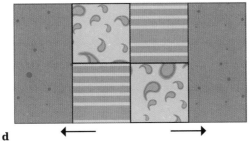

d

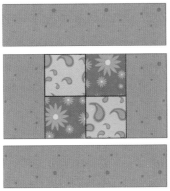
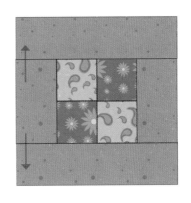

e

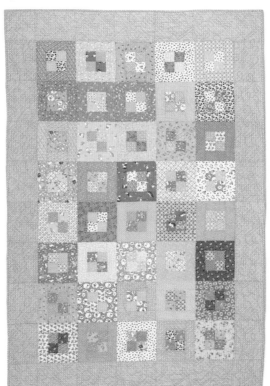

right:
Variation entitled A Quilt from Aunt Grace as all the Thirties fabrics came from one of the Aunt Grace collections designed by Judie Rothermel for Marcus Brothers. The quilt was pieced by Helen Allison and longarm quilted by The Quilt Room. When Helen sent her quilt to be quilted by The Quilt Room we knew we wanted to feature it in the book – it looked so totally different made up in these fabrics. She very kindly gave us permission and wouldn't let her cat Topsy curl up on it until it had been photographed!

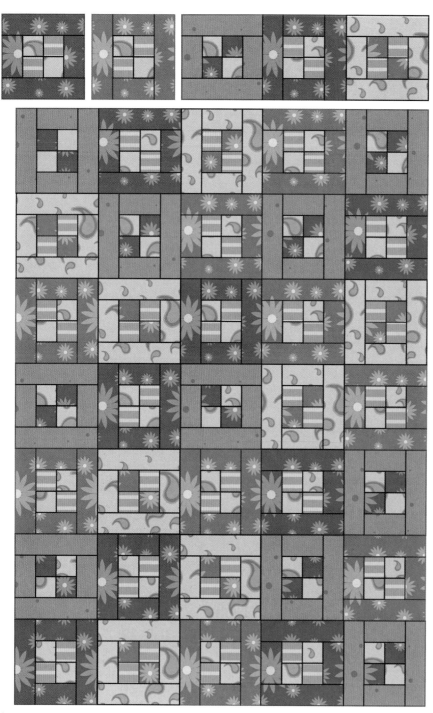

f

Putting your blocks together

Referring to diagram **f**, lay out the blocks into rows, rotating every other block 90 degrees. Make eight rows of five blocks. When you are happy with the layout, sew the blocks into rows and then sew the rows together.

Finishing the quilt

Join your six 6½in wide border strips into one continuous length and, referring to the instructions on page 122, add the borders to your quilt. Your quilt top is now complete. Quilt as desired and bind to finish.

|0 |½ |1 |1½ |2 |

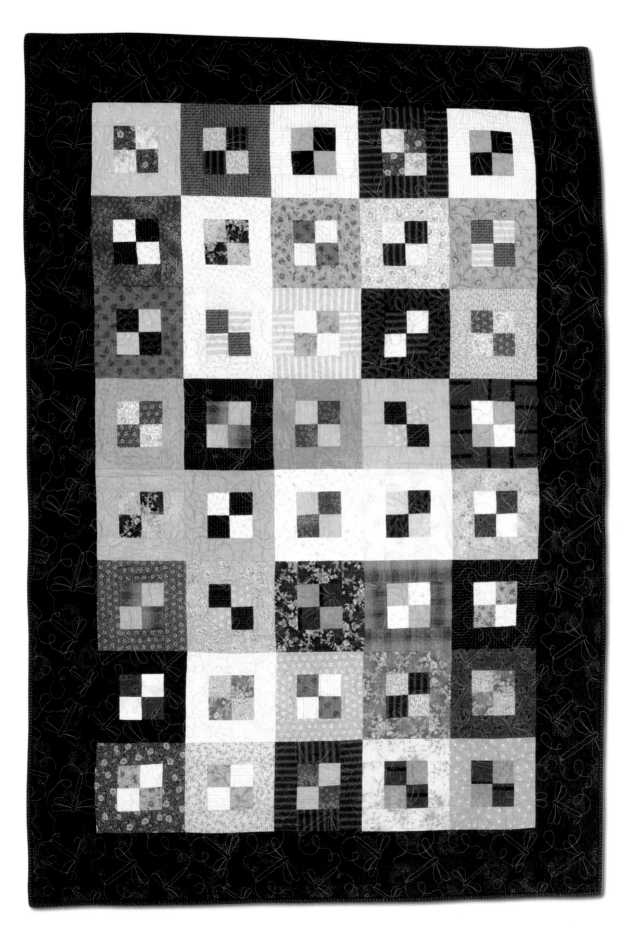

Log Cabin Hidden Stars

Vital statistics

Quilt size: 60 x 60in.
Block size: 14in.
Number of blocks: 16.
Setting: 4 x 4 blocks plus 2in wide border.

What you need

- One jelly roll or 40 2½in wide strips cut across the width of the fabric. Divide into 18 light and 22 dark, or 18 strips in one colour and 22 in another.

- 60cm (23½in) fabric for centres and stars.

- 50cm (20in) fabric for borders.

- 50cm (20in) fabric for binding.

When thinking of patterns using strips, the log cabin design comes to mind immediately. How could we possibly leave it out? Any jelly roll could be divided roughly into lights and darks and made up into a log cabin quilt. Here we have added the sparkle of a hidden star. It is not a difficult pattern but the last couple of logs in every block requires a bit of thought!

Our festive quilt is made up in the sumptuous country reds and greens from designer Terry Clothier Thompson. We chose a white fabric with a tiny gold spot for our hidden stars.

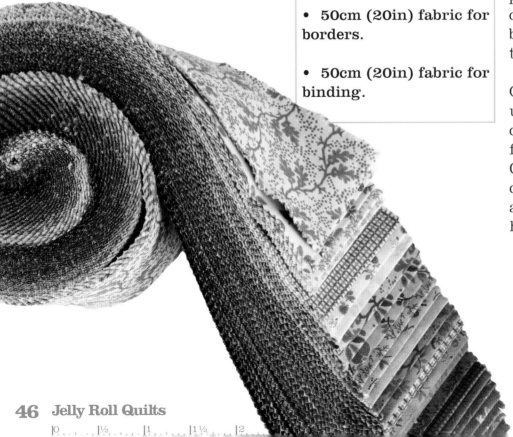

opposite:
The log cabin design is given an extra lift by the addition of the stars. The quilt was pieced by the authors and longarm quilted by The Quilt Room.

Cutting instructions

Centres and stars: Cut eight 2½in wide strips and then sub-cut into 124 2½in squares.

Strips: Cut the following rectangles (logs) from the jelly roll strips, cutting the longest first.

18 light strips:

12 of	2½ x 12½in
20 of	2½ x 10½in
16 of	2½ x 8½in
16 of	2½ x 6½in
16 of	2½ x 4½in
16 of	2½ x 2½in

22 dark strips:

16 of	2½ x 12½in
32 of	2½ x 10½in
16 of	2½ x 8½in
16 of	2½ x 6½in
16 of	2½ x 4½in

Borders: Cut into six 2½in wide strips across the width of the fabric.

Binding: Cut into six 2½in wide strips across the width of the fabric.

• Use a scant ¼in seam allowance throughout.

Sewing the blocks

1. Take a light square and a centre square (shown here as white) and with right sides together, sew together. Press away from centre. Sew a light 2½ x 4½in log to this unit. Press to outer log in direction of arrow (see diagram **a**).

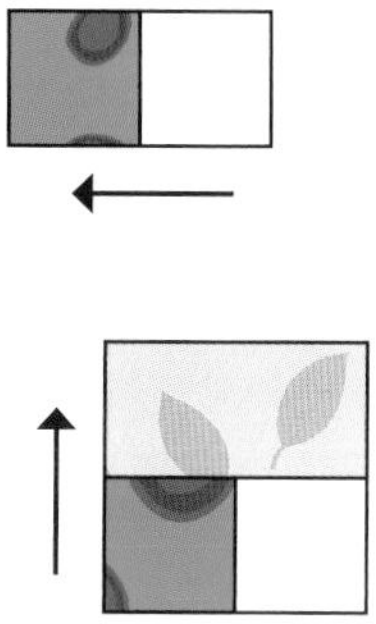

2. Sew a dark 2½ x 4½in log and press to outer log. Sew a dark 2½ x 6½in log and press to outer log (see diagram **b**).

3. Sew a light 2½ x 6½in log and press to outer log. Sew a light 2½ x 8½in log and press to outer log (see diagram **c**).

4. Sew a dark 2½ x 8½in log and press to outer log. Sew a dark 2½ x 10½in log and press to outer log (see diagram **d**).

All the blocks up to this point are the same and chain piecing will speed up the construction. When chain piecing, cut the threads and press before adding the next round of logs. Make 16 blocks.

a

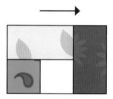

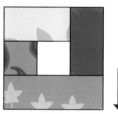

b

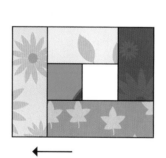

c

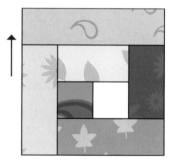

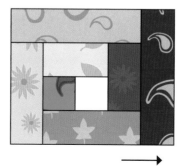

d

Tip

Keep your sewing at a constant speed. Chain piecing is a great way to speed up piecing but don't feel as though you have to have your foot flat on the pedal all the time. Sewing too fast can produce uneven stitches so a steady pace is preferable and will produce much neater work.

4 corner blocks

blocks 6, 7, 10 & 11

blocks 3, 5 12 & 14

blocks 2, 8, 9 & 15

e

Adding the last round of logs

The last round of logs varies and you need four different kinds of blocks to create the hidden stars, which are numbered to make the layout easier (see diagram **e**).

Sewing corner blocks 1, 4, 13, 16

• Add a 10½in light log and a 12½in light log as before and press seams as indicated by arrows in diagram **f**.

• The next 12½in dark log requires a star point. Lay a star square right sides together on the dark log and sew across the diagonal. Flip the square over. Press towards the star fabric and trim the excess. Make sure you have placed the star point in the correct place before cutting the excess (see diagram **g**).

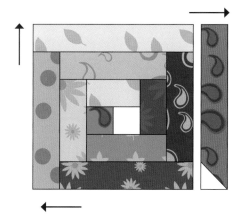

f

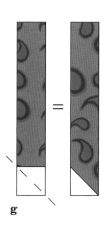

g

Tip

You really have very little wastage from a jelly roll, so don't be too zealous when trimming selvedges.

• Sew a star point to the next 12½in log and press open. Sew a star square to one end of it and press, as shown in diagram **h**.

Sewing centre blocks 6, 7, 10, 11

Referring to diagram **i**, add star points and star squares and press as shown. Make four of these blocks.

Sewing blocks 3, 5, 12, 14

Referring to diagram **j**, add star points and star squares and press. Make four of these blocks.

Sewing blocks 2, 8, 9, 15

Referring to diagram **k**, add star points and star squares and press. Make four of these blocks.

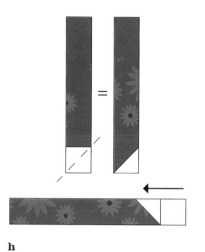

h

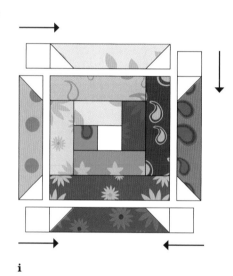

i

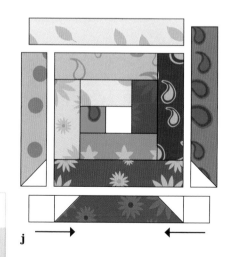

j

k

Tip

When butting seams together in machine piecing, try to have the top seam facing the foot of your machine and the bottom seam facing you.

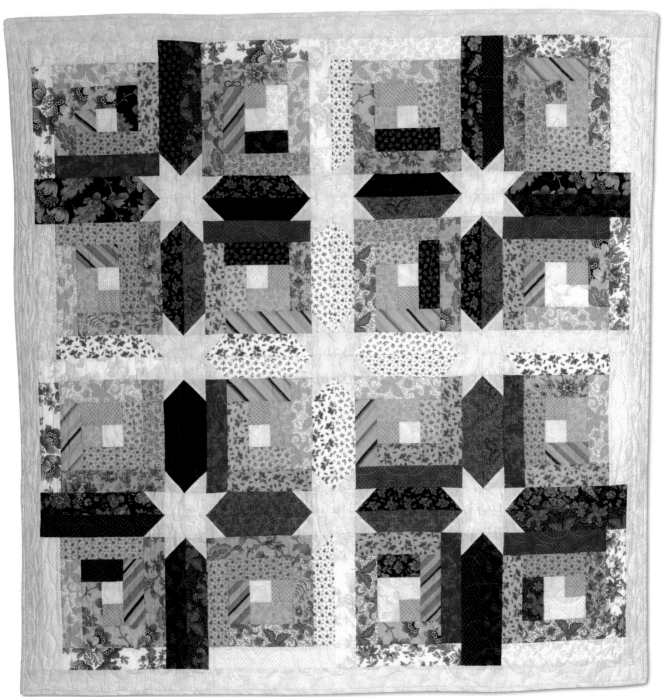

above:
Utopia seemed an appropriate name for this variation as the range of fabrics from Moda is called Shangri-La. It was pieced by Gwen Jones of The Quilt Room and longarm quilted by The Quilt Room.

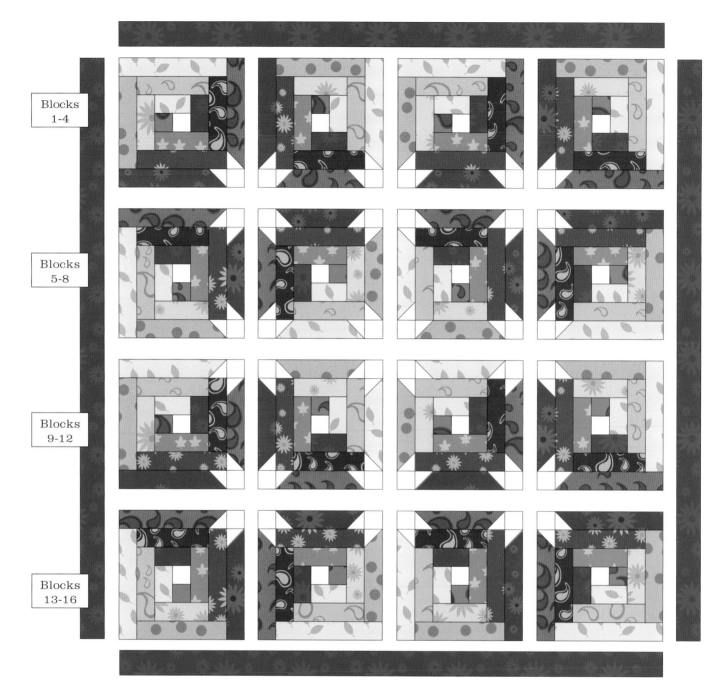

1

Joining the blocks

Now you have completed 16 blocks you
are ready to lay them out, referring
to diagram **1**. Block numbers start at
the top left and go across 1 to 4, the
second row starts 5 to 8, third row 9 to
12 and the bottom row 13 to 16. When
you have made sure they are in the
correct place, sew the blocks together,
matching seams.

Finishing the quilt

Join your six 2½in wide border
strips into one continuous length
and, referring to the instructions
on page 122, add borders to
the quilt. Your quilt top is now
complete. Quilt as desired and
bind to finish.

0   ½   1   1½   2

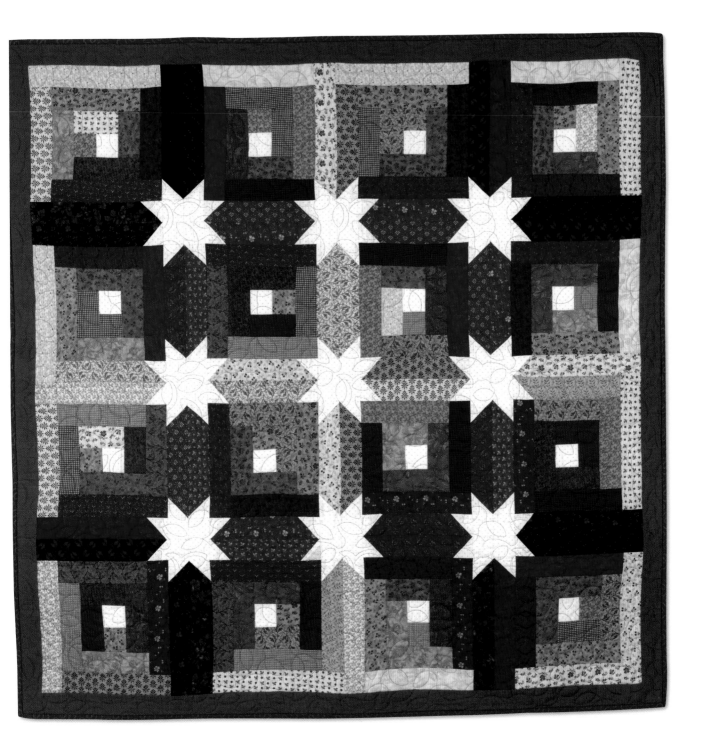

Spiral Strips

Vital statistics

Quilt size: 60 x 60in.
Block size: 16in.
Number of blocks: 9.
Setting: 3 x 3 blocks plus 6in border, or 7½in chequered border.

This is a great quilt to make as the fun really begins when you have completed your blocks and you lay them out to decide where they should go. Just by turning the blocks in different directions you open up endless possibilities. One technique, many variations.

We love the creamy country colours that Fig Tree Quilts include in their ranges and we thought this was our favourite among them, until we saw their next range and couldn't wait to get started on a quilt using that. It does become quite obsessive – be warned!

What you need

- One jelly roll or 40 assorted 2½in strips, cut across the width of the fabric – half light and half dark.

- 1.25m (49in) fabric for the border.

- 50cm (20in) of fabric for binding.

opposite:
The finished Spiral Strips quilt. We could have created many different looks just by turning the blocks around. The quilt was pieced by the authors and longarm quilted by The Quilt Room.

Cutting instructions

Borders: Don't cut these until you are ready to add them and have decided whether to insert a chequered border (see page 60).

Binding: Cut into seven 2½in wide strips across the width of the fabric.

• Use a scant ¼in seam allowance throughout.

Sewing quarter squares

1. Make a strip unit by sewing two light and two dark strips together, alternating dark and light (see diagram **a**). Press the seams to the dark fabric. The unit should measure 8½in. If not, check your seam allowance is a scant ¼in. Make a second strip unit in the same way.

2. Take the two strip units and lay them right sides together, reversing the order so that a light strip is lying on a dark strip. The seams will nest together nicely (see diagram **b**).

3. Trim the selvedge and sub-cut into 8½in squares. You should get four across the strip unit, as in diagram **c**.

4. Separate the squares carefully, keeping them on the cutting mat, and cut across the diagonal of each, always in the same direction (see diagram **d**). If you are right-handed you will find it easier to cut from the bottom right to the top left.

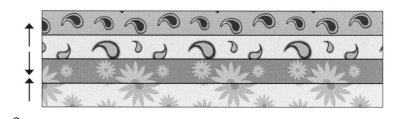

a

b

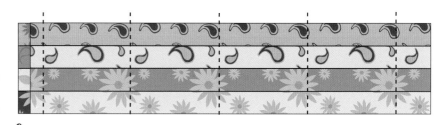

c

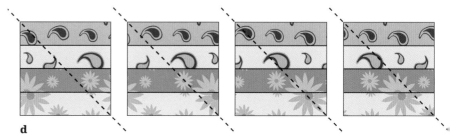

d

Tip

Make sure you keep the same layout with all your strip units, so always keep the bottom strip unit with the light strip to the top and your top strip unit with the light strip to the bottom.

|0 |½ |1 |1 ½ |2 |

5. You now have to stitch the layered triangles together along the diagonal. As these are bias edges, it is best to handle the fabric as little as possible. Carefully pick up a set of triangles one at a time and take them straight to the sewing machine. As all your seams are pressed to the dark side, the seams nest together perfectly. You could put a pin in to stop any movement. Sew along the diagonal as shown in diagram **e**.

6. Open to reveal your quarter squares and press (see diagram **f**). Repeat with your other layered triangles so that you have eight quarter squares completed.

7. Place four of the quarter squares together to see how they look, but do not sew them together at this stage (see diagram **g**). Repeat the procedure with your other strips to create 40 quarter squares in total. You will have four spare, which can be cut up and used for a chequered border (see page 60).

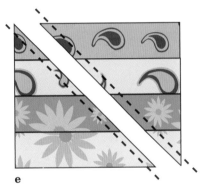

e

f

g

Tip

Take care when dealing with bias edges. Try not to pull them about too much as they will stretch.

Tip

It is best to sew all your quarter squares before deciding on the final arrangement.

Sewing your blocks together

1. Lay out all your quarter squares to decide on a pleasing arrangement. Once you are happy, sew them into blocks and then sew the blocks into rows. Finally, join the rows (see diagram **h**).

2. The quarter squares can be joined in lots of different ways. In diagram **i** the layout twists the upper right and bottom left squares in each block, which spins the blocks in a different way. You can have fun playing with different layouts.

h

i

|0 |½ |1 |1½ |2 |

Tip

It is okay to have narrow pieces in your chequered border but it looks better if you make sure you have complete squares in the corners.

Adding your borders

Now is the time to decide whether you wish to add one wide border or whether you want to insert a chequered border made up from the offcuts. If you want a plain border, cut your border fabric into six 6½in wide strips across the width of the fabric. Sew into one continuous length and, referring to the instructions on page 122, add the borders to your quilt.

If inserting a chequered border (see diagram **j**), cut your border fabric into six 3in wide strips cut across the width of the fabric and six 3½in wide strips cut across the width of the fabric.

Take the 3in wide strips and join to form one continuous length. Sew to the quilt as described on page 122.

To make the chequered border, gather up the offcuts and cut into 2½in wide segments. Join into a continuous length. You need at least 222in.

Measure the quilt and sew on the chequered border as before. Take the 3½in wide strips and join to form one continuous length. Measure the quilt as before and sew the border as for the plain version above.

Your quilt top is now complete. Quilt as desired and bind to finish.

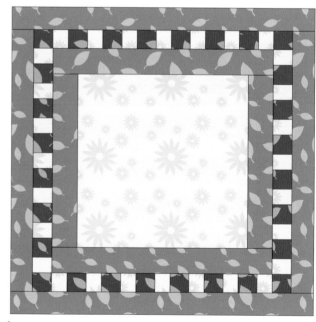

j

0   ½   1   1½   2

above:
The variation, Plum Pie, in a range by April Cornell was pieced by the authors and longarm quilted by The Quilt Room. After Pam had made the first version, Nicky very cleverly kept the offcuts and inserted the chequered border – so absolutely no wastage.

Daisy Chain

Vital statistics

Quilt size: 68 x 88in.
Throw size: 47 x 68in.
Block size: 10in.
Blocks per quilt: 48
Blocks per throw: 24
Setting for quilt: 6 x 8 blocks plus 3in wide border.
Setting for throw: 4 x 6 blocks plus 3in wide border.

What you need

For the quilt:
• 1½ jelly rolls or 60 assorted 2½in strips cut across the width of fabric.

• 2m (79in) background and border fabric.

• 60cm (23½in) for binding (if not using strips from a jelly roll).

For the throw:
• Three quarters of a jelly roll or 30 assorted 2½in strips, cut to the width of the fabric.

• 1.25m (49in) background and border fabric.

• 50cm (20in) for binding (if not using strips from a jelly roll).

This was one of those occasions when one jelly roll wasn't enough – we just wanted to keep going. Using 40 strips gave an asymmetrical look to the design and although 30 was a good size for a throw, we felt the gorgeous, fresh colours from Heather Bailey's range really did lend themselves to a larger quilt.

In the end, we decided to use half of another roll as having 20 strips left over just gave us more options. We could have added a further border to make the quilt even bigger, or we could have made the handy Quilt Carry Bag on page 116. As it happened, we used some of the strips to bind the quilt and kept some for swapping!

We have given instructions here for the throw as well (these are in brackets throughout). This makes up really quickly and, in bright, sunny colours, would make a lovely first bed quilt as a special present for a child, as shown in the variation on page 67.

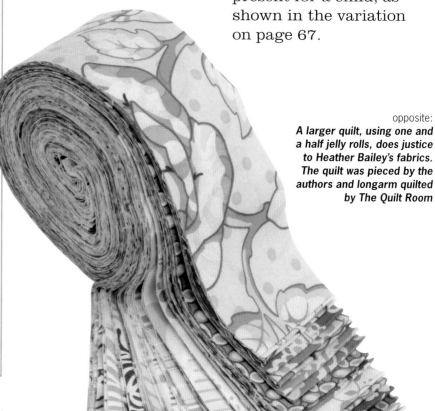

opposite:
A larger quilt, using one and a half jelly rolls, does justice to Heather Bailey's fabrics. The quilt was pieced by the authors and longarm quilted by The Quilt Room

Cutting instructions

Strips: All strips should be cut in half to create 120 (60) strips, half the width of the fabric.

Background fabric: First cut six (three) 4½in wide strips across the width of the fabric. Cut these in half to create 12 (six) 4½in wide, half-width strips. Next cut six (three) 2½in wide strips across the width of the fabric. Cut these in half to create 12 (six) 2½in wide, half-width strips.

Borders: Cut eight (six) 3½in wide strips across the width of the background fabric for borders.

Binding: Cut nine (six) 2½in wide strips across the width of the fabric. If you are using strips from a jelly roll, then this is not necessary.

After cutting the fabric, make three separate piles:
Fabric strips.
2½in background strips.
4½in background strips.

• Use a scant ¼in seam allowance throughout.

This quilt requires you to create three different strip units, A, B and C, which will form the blocks.

Sewing strip unit A

1. Choose five fabric strips and sew them into strip unit A as per diagram **a**. Do not spend too much time on your selection. A good policy is to use what is next in the pile unless it is just too similar. Press the seams as shown by arrows. The measurement of this strip unit should be 10½in. If not, adjust your seam allowance. Repeat to create a total of six (three) strip unit As.

2. Lay one strip unit A on the cutting mat at a time. Trim the selvedge and sub-cut into eight 2½in segments (see diagram **b**). Always line up the markings on the ruler with the seams to make sure you are cutting at a right angle. You need 48 (24) unit A segments in total.

a

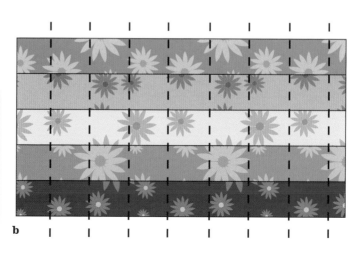

b

Tip

The secret of success with this quilt is pressing the seams in the right direction. If you do that, they nest together nicely, making it much easier to match seams.

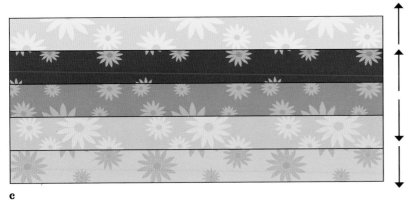

c

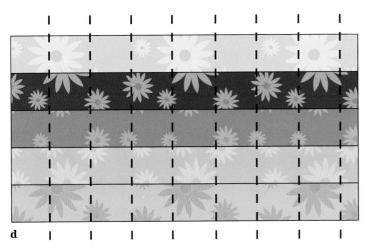

d

Sewing strip unit B

3. Choose four fabric strips and one 2½in background strip and sew them into strip unit B as shown in diagram **c**. Press the seams as shown. Repeat to create a total of twelve (six) strip unit Bs.

4. Lay one strip unit B on the cutting mat at a time. Trim selvedge and sub-cut into eight 2½in segments in just the same way as for strip unit A (see diagram **d**). You need 96 (48) unit B segments in total.

Sewing strip unit C

5. Choose three fabric strips and one 4½in background strip and sew them into strip unit C as shown in diagram **e**. Press the seams as shown. Repeat to create a total of twelve (six) strip unit Cs.

6. Lay one strip unit C on the cutting mat at a time. Trim the selvedge and sub-cut into eight 2½in segments, just as you did for strip units A and B (see diagram **f**). You need 96 (48) unit C segments in total.

7. Put unit A, unit B and unit C segments into three piles, making sure the background fabric always faces the same way.

e

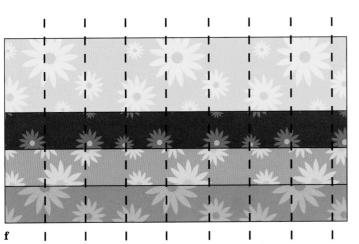

f

unit A   **unit B**   **unit C**

Tip

Do not try to save time by cutting more than one strip unit at a time. You will be in trouble later if you do not cut at a right angle.

Making your blocks

1. Sew unit B and unit C together, matching the seams. Make sure unit C is on the left, as shown in diagram **g**. The seams will nest together nicely. Try to have different fabrics next to each other. Repeat to use up all units B and C. You need 96 (48). Press the seams to unit C, as shown.

2. Turn half of these round so that the background fabrics of the units are at the bottom and place unit A in the centre (see diagram **h**). Again, it works best if you have different fabrics next to each other.

3. Sew together, matching the seams. Press the seams away from the centre. You need 48 (24) blocks. They should measure 10½in square (see diagram **i**).

unit C unit B

g ←

unit C unit B   unit A   unit B unit C

h

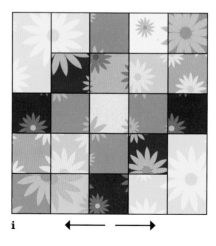

i ←   →

opposite:
Variation of Daisy Chain in a sunny range of yellow and blue fabrics by April Cornell. With a crisp, white background fabric, this smaller quilt is ideal as a throw or for a child's bed. The quilt was pieced by Kath Bock of Southill Piecemakers, Cornwall and longarm quilted by The Quilt Room.

0   ½   1   1½   2

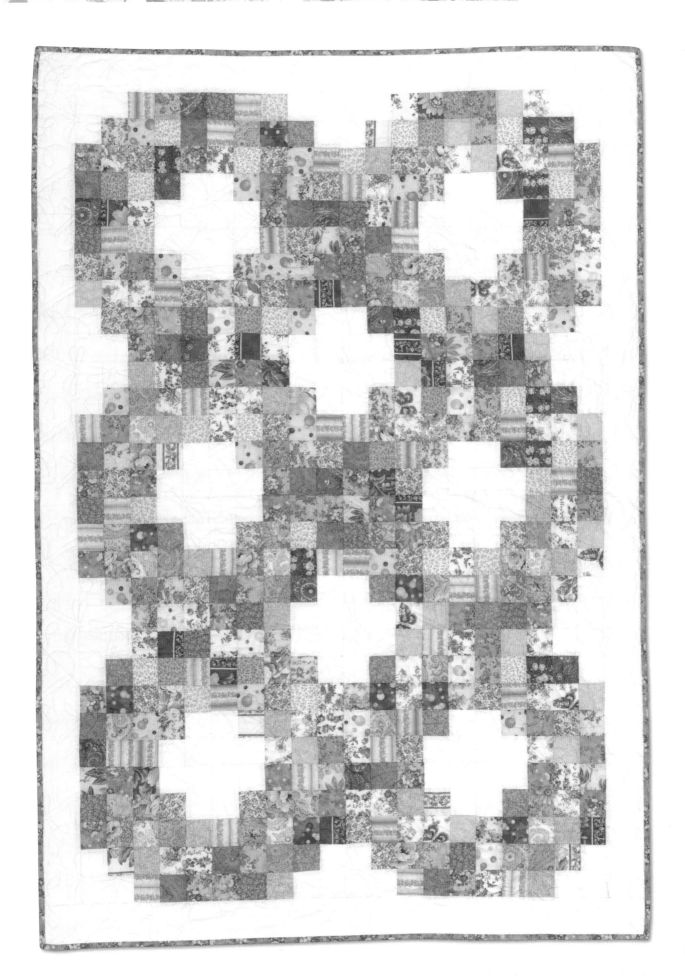

throw

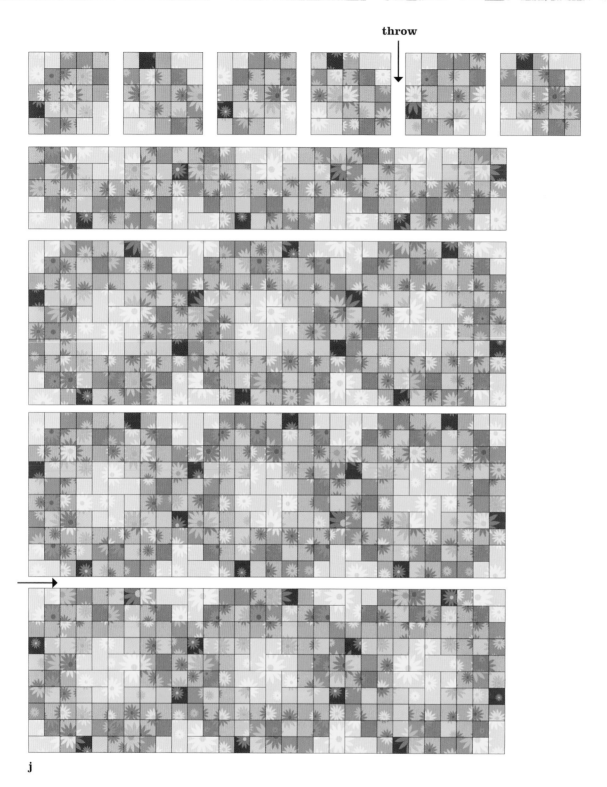

j

Putting your blocks together

Referring to **diagram j**, lay out the blocks
for the rows, rotating every other block
90 degrees. Make six rows of four blocks
for the throw and eight rows of six blocks
for the quilt. When you are happy with
the layout, sew blocks into rows and then
sew rows together.

Finishing the quilt

Join your eight (six) 3½in wide
border strips into one continuous
length and, referring to the
instructions on page 122, add
the borders to your quilt. Your
quilt top is now complete. Quilt as
desired and bind to finish.

0   ½   1   1½   2

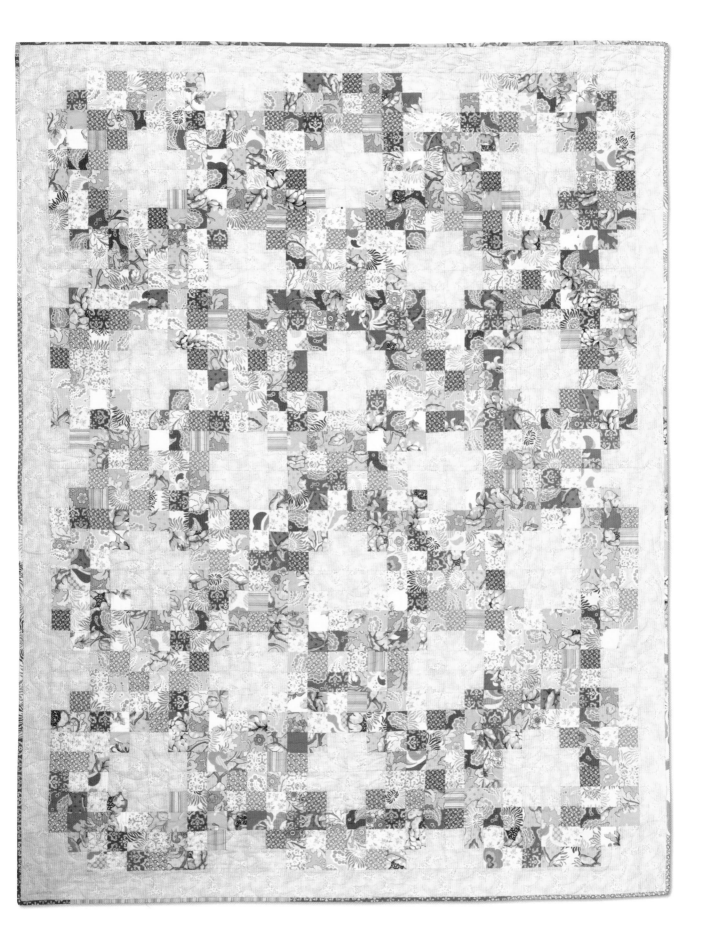

Floral Bouquet

Vital statistics
Quilt size: 60 x 88in.
Block size: 10in.
Number of blocks: 39.
Border: 2in.

A gorgeous range by Sandy Gervais is used in this bright, fresh quilt with a white-on-white background fabric, which sets it off to perfection. Although only one jelly roll is used, it makes up to a generous single bed size quilt. You could of course add an extra border to increase it to a double size very easily.

The variation called *Fossils in the Garden*, on page 76, shows the completely different effect created by using the same fabric in each flower.

What you need

• One jelly roll or 40 2½in wide floral strips cut the width of the fabric.

• 3.5 metres (138in) background fabric.

• The border is formed from the off-cuts from strips.

• 60cm (23½in) for binding.

opposite:
Floral Bouquet *uses a white background to set off Sandy Gervais's pretty fabrics. The quilt was pieced by Isabelle Ramage of Southill Piecemakers, Cornwall and longarm quilted by The Quilt Room.*

Cutting instructions

Binding: Cut binding fabric into eight 2½in wide strips across its width.

Floral strips: From each floral strip from the jelly roll cut the following:

One square	2½ x 2½in
One rectangle	2½ x 4½in
Two rectangles	2½ x 6½in
One rectangle	2½ x 8½in
One rectangle	2½ x 14in (set aside for border)

Background fabric: Cut 40 2½in wide strips across the width of the fabric and sub-cut each strip as follows:

Five squares	2½ x 2½in
One rectangle	2½ x 4½in
One rectangle	2½ x 8½in
One rectangle	2½ x 10½in

Then cut two 15¼in wide strips across the width of the background fabric and sub-cut into four 15¼in squares. From the balance of these strips, cut two 9in squares (see diagram **a**).

Cut across both diagonals of the 15¼in squares to form 16 setting triangles. Cut across one diagonal of the 9in squares to form four corner triangles. Cutting the setting and corner triangles this way ensures the outer edges of your quilt are not on the bias.

- Use a scant ¼in seam allowance throughout.

Tip

If you enjoy making quilts from jelly rolls, why not ensure you always have some 2½in strips handy by always cutting one 2½in strip from any new fabric you buy? You will accumulate an eclectic mix of strips that you can have great fun making into a quilt.

15¼" **x4**

9" **x2**

a

b

Sewing the blocks

The blocks are each made up of the units shown in diagram **c**. Speed up construction by chain piecing all the A units and then all the B units and so on to H. You need 39 of each unit. Keep them all in separate piles.

(A)

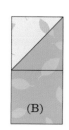
(B)

(C)

(D)

(E)

(F)

(G)

(H)

c

0 ⋯⋯ ½ ⋯⋯ 1 ⋯⋯ 1½ ⋯⋯ 2 ⋯⋯

Unit A: Take one background square and lay it right sides together on a 2½ x 6½in floral rectangle, as shown in the diagram for unit A.

For the first few strips, draw a diagonal line to mark the sewing line but after sewing a few you will probably find it unnecessary as you get your eye in. Sew across the diagonal. Flip the square over. Press towards the darker fabric and trim the excess. Unit A strips must have the background triangle on the top left.

Unit B: Repeat instructions for unit A but sew a background square on a 2½ x 4½in floral rectangle (see the diagram for unit B).

Unit C: Sew a 2½in floral square to a 2½in background square (see the diagram for unit C).

Unit E: Repeat instructions for Unit A but sew the background square in the other direction. Unit E strips must have the background triangle on the top right (see the diagram for unit E).

Unit F: Repeat instructions for unit E but sew a background square on a 2½ x 8½in floral rectangle (see the diagram for unit F).

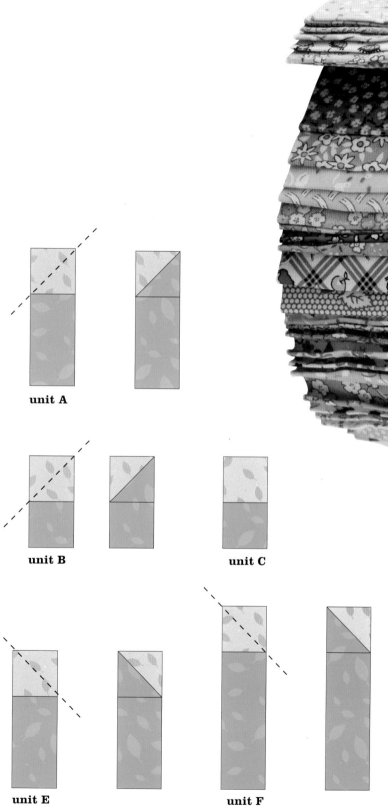

unit A

unit B   unit C

unit E   unit F

Assembling the blocks

1. Sew unit D to unit C as shown in diagram **1**.

2. Sew unit B as shown in diagram **2**.

3. Sew unit E to the bottom as shown in diagram **3**.

4. Sew unit A to the left side as shown in diagram **4**.

5. Sew unit F to the bottom as shown in diagram **5**.

6. Sew unit G to the left side as shown in diagram **6**.

7. Sew unit H to the bottom as shown in diagram **7**.

Repeat until you have made 39 blocks.

1   **2**

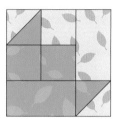

3

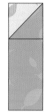
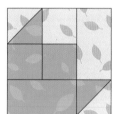
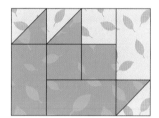

4

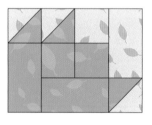
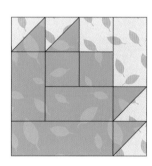

5

Tip

When you are doing a lot of sewing, have a small rectangle of scrap fabric by your machine and always run your machine onto it when you come to the end of your line of sewing. This remains under your pressser foot until you are ready to sew again and you therefore won't have to hang on to the ends of your thread when starting to sew. This will not only save you thread but the tension on your first few stitches will be neater.

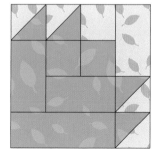
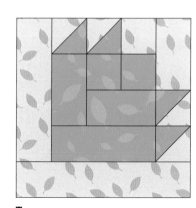

6   **7**

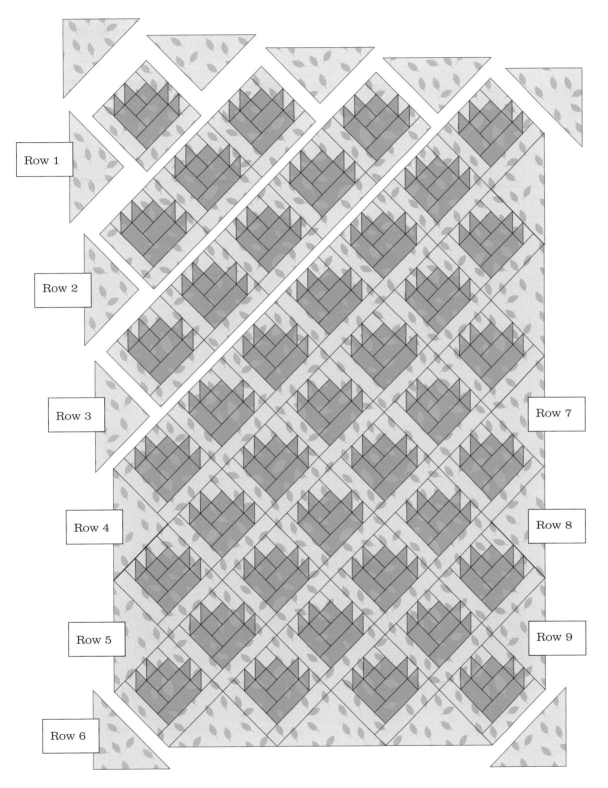

Row 1
Row 2
Row 3
Row 4
Row 5
Row 6
Row 7
Row 8
Row 9

Setting blocks on point

Referring to the diagram above, sew a
setting triangle to each side of a block
to create row 1. Following the diagram,
continue to sew the blocks together to
form rows with a setting triangle at each
end. Sew the corner triangles on last.

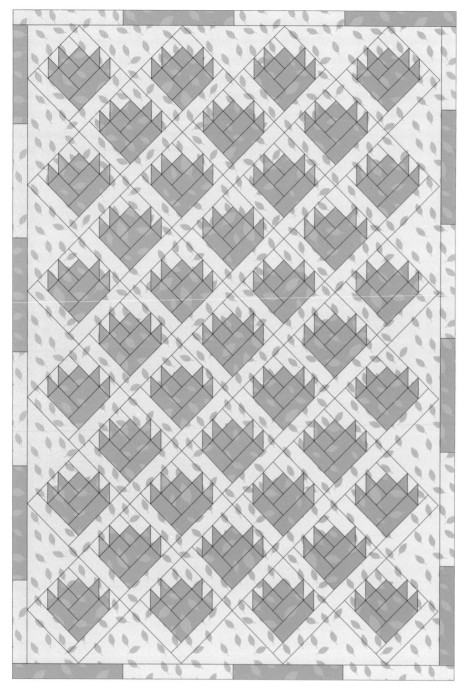

Sewing the borders

Select 22 of the 2½ x 14in border strips you cut from the jelly roll and sew together to form a long length. Determine the vertical measurement from top to bottom through the centre of your quilt top. Cut two side borders to this measurement. Sew these to the quilt.

Determine the horizontal measurement from side to side across the centre of the quilt top. Cut these two borders to this measurement. Sew to the quilt.

Your quilt top is now complete (see the diagram left). Quilt as desired and bind to finish.

above:

The variation of Floral Bouquet, *entitled* Fossils in the Garden, *is made from a tone-on-tone range called Fossil Fern. These fabrics combine beautifully with other fabrics but in this instance we felt it deserved a quilt of its own! In this quilt each flower is made from the same fabric to create a totally different effect and for the background we have used a pale grey Fossil Fern. It was pieced by the authors and longarm quilted by The Quilt Room.*

|0 |½ |1 |1½ |2 |

Friendship Braid

Vital statistics

Quilt size: 56 x 63in.
Setting: 8 braids of 40 trapezoids plus 6in wide border.

This beautiful quilt would enhance anyone's bedroom. The subtle colouring from the designer Anna Griffin blends together to create a sophisticated country cottage style quilt.

This quilt design normally has the lights and darks on either side of the braid more defined but here we have avoided such a strong contrast to create a much softer effect. For the more traditional style of using light and dark fabric, see our variation on page 81.

What you need

• One jelly roll or 40 2½in wide strips the width of the fabric (20 light and 20 dark). Note: Although our lights and darks were not clearly defined it is still necessary to separate them into two categories for cutting purposes.

• 1.1m (43in) for borders cut into six 6½in wide strips across the width of the fabric.

• 50cm (20in) for binding cut into seven 2½in wide strips across the width of the fabric.

our variation on page 81.

opposite:
Friendship Braid using subtle fabrics by Anna Griffin. This pattern also looks good with a sashing between each of the braids – another option to try. The quilt was pieced by the authors and longarm quilted by The Quilt Room.

This quilt requires the use of an Omnigrid 96L or similar triangle to cut 5in finished size trapezoids (see the Tools section on pages 120-121). This refers to the finished size of the longest side of the trapezoid. Whatever triangle you use, please lay it on the template below to make sure you know which markings on the triangle to follow.

• Use a scant ¼in seam allowance throughout.

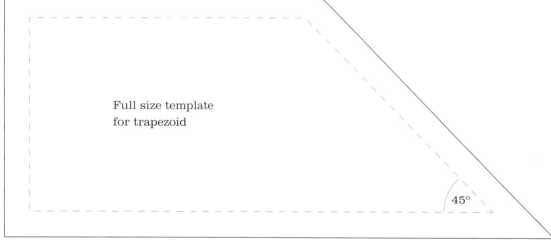

Full size template for trapezoid

45°

If you are using any triangle other than an Omnigrid 96L, please check your measurement with this full size template.

Cutting your strips

1. Trapezoids are needed from the dark fabrics and reverse trapezoids are needed from the light fabrics. You can cut a dark strip and a light strip together. Lay out a dark strip right side up and a light strip on top, right side down, and trim selvedge.

2. Place the triangle against the trimmed edge, using the correct markings for your ruler. Cut (see diagram **a**).

3. Rotate the triangle 180 degrees as shown in diagram **b** and cut.

4. Continue rotating the triangle and cutting. You should get eight trapezoids from the dark strip and eight reverse trapezoids from the light strip (see diagram **c**).

5. Continue cutting all your strips. Keep two separate piles: pile A for your dark trapezoids and pile B for your light reverse trapezoids. You will have 160 in each pile.

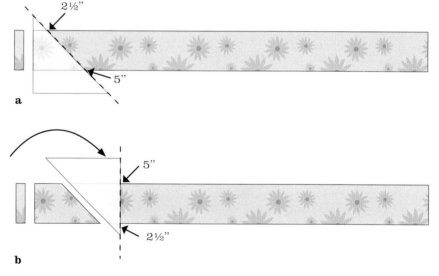

a

b

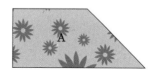
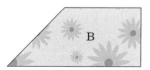

c

|0 |½ |1 |1½ |2 |

Constructing the braids

Once you get started on your braids this is an easy quilt to chain piece. You will have four braids starting with a light strip and four braids starting with a dark strip. The light strips will form the left hand side of the braid and the dark will form the right hand side. The braids are constructed from the bottom to the top.

1. First make a braid that starts with a light reverse trapezoid. Lay a dark trapezoid right sides together on a light reverse trapezoid and sew as shown in diagram **d**. Finger press open.

2. Add a light reverse trapezoid to the unit and continue adding lights and darks as shown in diagram **e**. The edges of the trapezoids will match at the bottom and will intersect at the seam line at the top. Finger press towards the piece you have just added until you finish a braid and then press gently, taking care not to stretch the bias edges. Trim the dog ears (as described on page 123). You need to make four braids of 40 trapezoids that start with a light reverse trapezoid.

3. Next you need to make four braids of 40 trapezoids that start with a dark trapezoid. Lay a light reverse trapezoid right sides together on a dark trapezoid and sew as shown in diagram **f**. Finger press open.

4. Add a dark trapezoid to the unit and continue adding lights and darks as shown in diagram **g**. Finger press until you finish a braid and then press gently, taking care not to stretch the bias edges. Trim the dog ears.

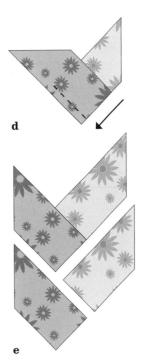

d

e

f

g

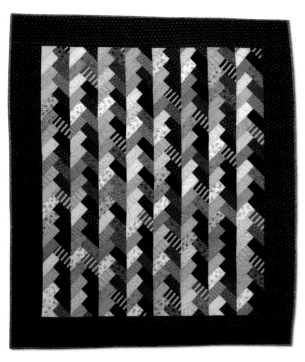

above:
Our variation, Inky's Quilt, pieced by the authors in an earthy range of taupes from Japan, shows the more traditional effect with the lights and darks on either side of the braid more defined. The quilt was longarm quilted by The Quilt Room.

Tip

You can photocopy the template and stick it to the triangle you are using (if not an Omnigrid 96L) to ensure you use the correct markings.

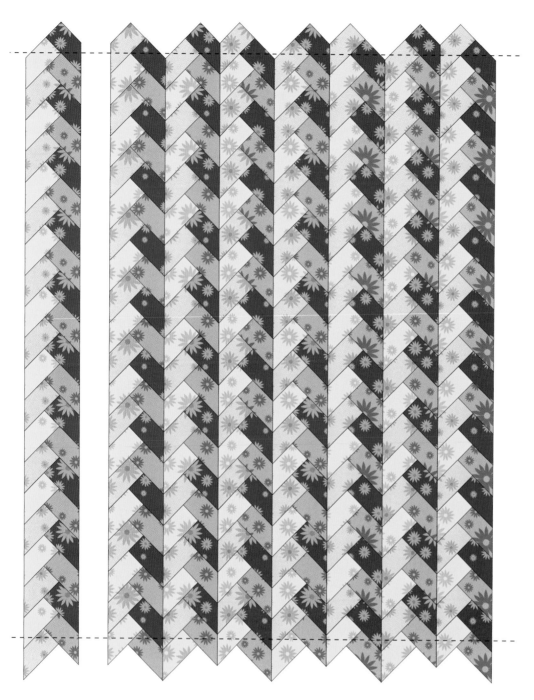

h

Joining the braids

Sew your eight columns together, alternating the ones starting with a light fabric and the ones starting with a dark. Pin at the seam intersections to ensure perfect matches. Handle the edges carefully to ensure they don't stretch out of shape. Trim the top and bottom to square the quilt top (see diagram **h**).

Finishing the quilt

Join your six 6½in wide border strips into one continuous length and, referring to the instructions on page 122, add borders to the quilt. Your quilt top is now complete. Quilt as desired and bind to finish.

|0 |½ |1 |1½ |2 |

Pineapple Surprise

Vital statistics

Quilt size: 54 x 66in (bonus quilt 42 x 60in).
Block size: 12in.
Number of blocks: 20.
Setting: 4 x 5 blocks plus 3in wide border.

It is probably the Scottish blood that runs through our family, but we love the fact that for very little extra effort you can end up with a second quilt, shown on pages 90-91. This really feels like getting value for money!

Apart from one jelly roll, this quilt uses 100 4½in neutral squares. Now these don't take too long to cut but for extra speed and variety we used the ready-cut 4½in squares in a neutral Charm Pack.

We chose a basic red jelly roll containing a mixture of orange-reds through to deep burgundies. When mixed with the neutral squares, it turned out to have a lovely rustic effect. The 'bonus' quilt, with its wide sashing, is ideal to show off some fancy quilting.

What you need

- One jelly roll or 40 2½in wide red strips cut the width of the fabric.

- 1.5m (59in) neutral fabric.

- 60cm (23½in) border fabric.

- 50cm (20in) binding fabric.

opposite:
With its lovely warm colours, Pineapple Surprise is a great quilt for curling up under on a cold winter's evening. The quilt was pieced by the authors and longarm quilted by The Quilt Room.

Cutting instructions

Strips: Cut each strip into the following rectangles:
one 2½ x 4½in
two 2½ x 8½in
one 2½ x 12½in
Organise your rectangles into piles.
You will have a pile of:
40 2½ x 4½in rectangles
80 2½ x 8½in rectangles
40 2½ x 12½in rectangles

Neutral fabric: Cut 12 4½in strips and sub-cut into 100 4½in squares.

Border: Cut six 3½in wide strips the width of the fabric.

Binding: Cut seven 2½in wide strips width of the fabric.

Tip

We always use a scant ¼in seam allowance throughout except when sewing the second diagonal line in diagram **c** where we use a generous ¼in seam allowance. Ideally, you should be sewing a ⅛in seam allowance to give you a ¼in seam allowance after cutting. This would make your bonus triangle much smaller.

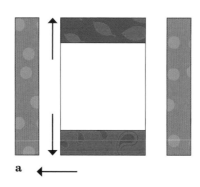

a

b

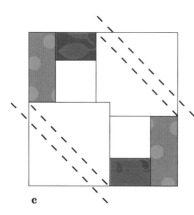

c

Sewing your blocks

1. Choose two 4½in rectangles and sew to top and bottom of a square. Press seams to rectangles. Choose two 8½in rectangles and sew to either side. Press seams to rectangles (see diagram **a**). Choose different fabrics for a scrappy effect.

2. Take two neutral squares and draw a diagonal line from corner to corner on the reverse (see diagram **b**). This is your stitching guide. Place the squares on two opposite corners of your block and stitch on the marked line as shown in diagram **c**.

3. When you have stitched along the diagonal to join the corner squares to the block, stitch another line parallel using a generous ¼in seam allowance (see diagram **c**). You can then cut off the excess fabric by carefully cutting between the parallel lines.

4. You now have two ready-sewn half-square 'bonus' triangles to use for the bonus quilt on pages 90-91 (see diagram **d**).

5. Press the corners of the block open (see diagram **e**).

6. Choose two 8½in rectangles and sew to the top and bottom of the block. Press seams to rectangles. Then choose two 12½in rectangles and sew to either side. Press seams to rectangles (see diagram **f**).

7. Take two more squares and draw a diagonal line from corner to corner on the reverse as before. Place them on the two opposite corners and stitch on the marked line. Stitch the parallel line as before (see diagram **g**).

8. When you cut between the two lines you will have created two more bonus triangles (see diagram **h**).

9. Now you've got the idea, you can start chain-piecing to speed up the sewing. You need 20 blocks, as shown in diagram **i**.

d

h

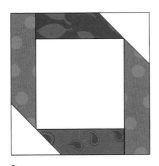

e

i

f

g

Tip

The blade on your rotary cutter will eventually become dull. If you notice that it takes more pressure to cut, or if it misses a few threads when cutting, then it is time to change the blade. You will be amazed at the difference it makes. Take care when changing the blade, carefully laying out the pieces in the correct order so you know exactly how to put them back together.

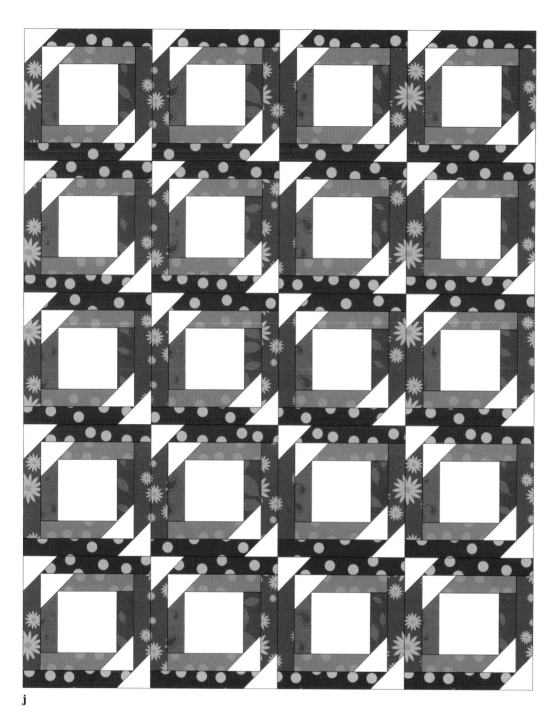

j

Sewing your blocks together

Referring to diagram **j**, join the blocks together, four across and five down.

Finishing the quilt

Join your six 3½in wide border strips into one continuous length and, referring to the instructions on page 122, add borders to the quilt. Your quilt top is now complete. Quilt as desired and bind to finish.

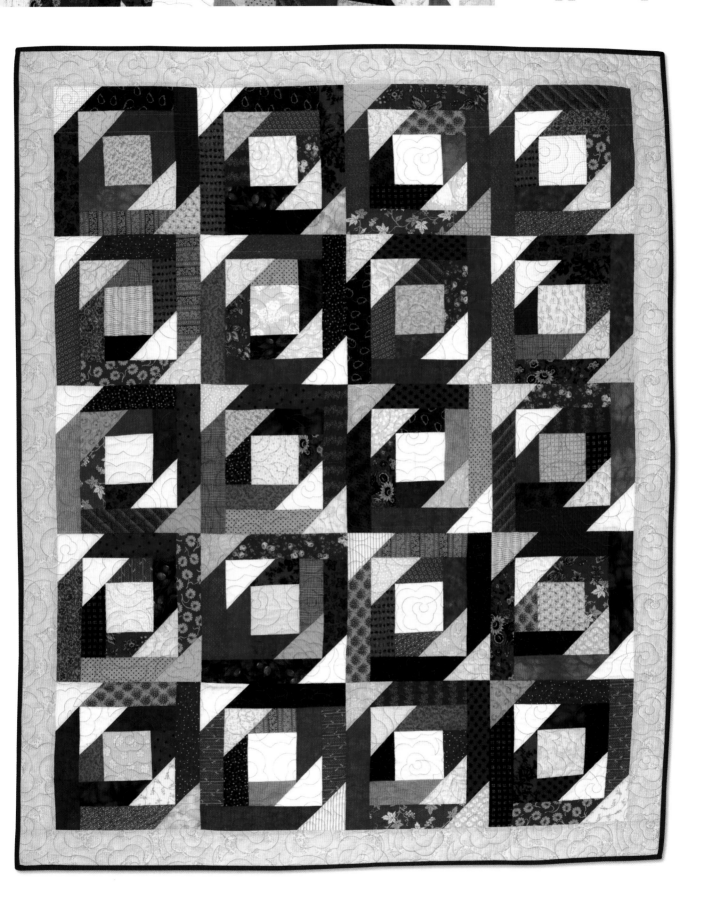

Making the bonus quilt

1. Press and resize the bonus triangles to 3½in square.

2. From your sashing and border fabric, cut five 6½in wide strips down the length of the fabric.

3. Join bonus triangles into four strip rows of 20 triangles each.

4. Measure each strip row and cut sashing to the shortest length.

5. Sew strips and sashing together as shown in the diagram, easing if necessary.

6. Quilt as desired and bind to finish.

What you need

- **80 bonus triangles, as described in *Pineapple Surprise* instructions.**

- **1.6m (63in) sashing and border fabric.**

- **50cm (20in) binding fabric.**

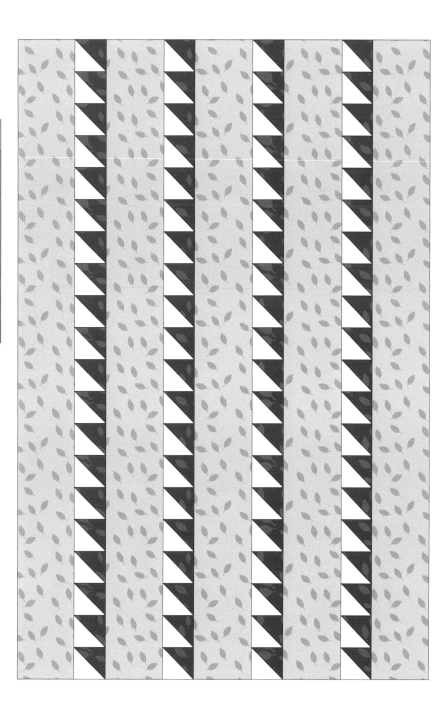

|0 |½ |1 |1½ |2

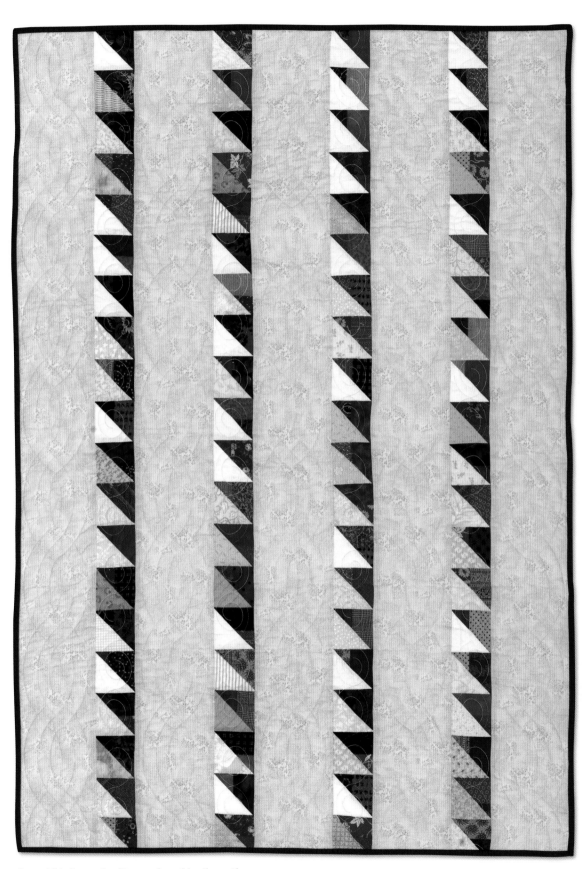

above: *This 'bonus' quilt was pieced by the authors and longarm quilted by The Quilt Room. There is absolutely no wastage when the excess triangles can be used up in another quilt like this.*

Twin Stars

Vital statistics

Quilt size: 52 x 68in.
Block size: 8in.
Number of blocks: 35.
Setting: 5 x 7 blocks plus 6in wide border.

To obtain the best effect with this quilt you do need to have several different colours, so spend time sorting through your jelly roll to make sure you have enough variety and to decide how to allocate your strips.

This is the only quilt in the book where we have used half-square triangles and once you learn how to create them from 2½in strips, it opens up a whole new world of many more exciting quilts.

To make a finished 2in square composed of two half-square triangles you would normally need to cut triangles from a square of 2⅞ in cut in half diagonally. As we are working with 2½in strips we have to rethink how to cut these triangles. It is absolutely no problem with the right tool. We used the Omnigrid 96 triangle or the larger version 96L (see Tools on page 120).

opposite:
It is well worth learning the technique for making half-square triangles as it opens up so many design possibilities from a jelly roll. Twin Stars was pieced by the authors and longarm quilted by The Quilt Room.

What you need

- One jelly roll or 40 2½in strips cut across the width of the fabric divided as follows:

Eight colour 1 (aqua) for the flying geese blocks.
Eight colour 2 (red) for the flying geese blocks.
Six colour 3 (pink) for the half-square triangles.
Six light for the half-square triangles.

Three medium for the four patch blocks.
Three dark for the four patch blocks.
Five light for the corner squares on star two.

- 1.25m (49in) cream background for the flying geese blocks.

- 1.1m (43in) for the border.

- 50cm (20in) fabric for binding.

Cutting instructions

Colour 1 (aqua): cut each of the eight strips into nine rectangles 2½ x 4½in. You need 72 in total.

Colour 2 (red): Cut each of the eight strips into 17 2½in squares. You need a strip 42½in long so do not over-trim the selvedge. You need 136 in total.

Light strips for corner squares of star two: Cut five light strips into 68 2½in squares.

Cream background fabric: Cut into 17 2½in strips across the width of the fabric. Take nine of these and cut into 2½in squares. You should get 16 per strip. You need 144 2½in squares. Take the remaining eight and cut into 2½ x 4½in rectangles. You should get nine from each strip. You need 68 rectangles measuring 2½ x 4½in.

Borders: Cut into six 6½in wide strips across the width of the fabric.

Binding: Cut into six 2½in wide strips across the width of the fabric.

• Use a scant ¼in seam allowance throughout.

This quilt requires the use of the Omnigrid 96 or 96L to make half-square triangles from a 2½in wide strip. If you are using a specialist triangle other than an Omnigrid, which allows you to cut half square triangles from 2½in wide strips, please photocopy this template and lay it on your triangle to ensure you are using the correct markings.

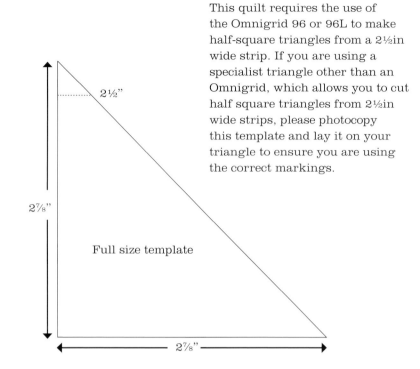

2½"

2⅞"

2⅞"

Full size template

|0 |½ |1 |1 ½ |2

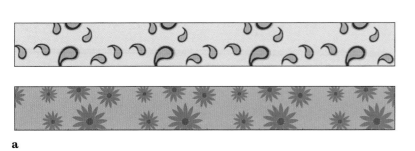

a

b

c

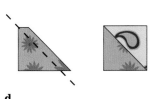

d

Sewing half-square triangle units for star block one

1. Press one colour 3 (pink) and one light strip (see diagram **a**) right sides together ensuring that they are exactly one on top of the other. The pressing will help hold the two strips together. Lay out on cutting mat and trim selvedge on left side.

2. Position the Omnigrid 96 as shown in diagram **b**, lining up the 2in mark at the bottom edge of the strips, and cut the first triangle. You will notice that the cut out triangle has a flat top. This would just have been a dog ear you needed to cut off so you have saved some time!

3. Rotate the Omnigrid 96 180 degrees to the right as shown in diagram **c** and cut the next triangle. Continue along the strip. You will get 25 sets of triangles from one strip.

4. Sew along the diagonals to form 25 half-square triangles. Trim all dog ears and press open (see diagram **d**).

5. Repeat with the other five pink and five light strips. You need 144 half-square triangles in total.

Tip

When pressing the half-square triangles you would normally press to the pink. However, if you press 36 to the lighter fabric and keep in a separate pile to be used for making the centre blocks, the seams will nest together nicely.

Sewing flying geese units for star block one

1. Take one cream background 2½in square and lay it right sides together on a 2½ x 4½in colour 1 (aqua) rectangle. Sew across the diagonal as shown in diagram **e**. If it helps, draw the diagonal line in first to mark your stitching line.

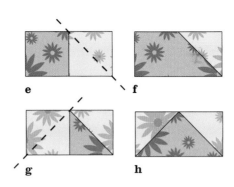

e   f

g   h

2. Flip the square over and press towards the background fabric (see diagram **f**). Trim the excess background fabric but do not trim the aqua fabric. Although this creates a little more bulk, this aqua rectangle keeps your flying geese in shape.

3. Place a second background 2½in square and lay it on the other side as shown in diagram **g** and sew across the diagonal. Flip the square over and press as before.

4. Trim excess background fabric. Repeat the whole process to make 72 units as in diagram **h**.

Assembling star block one

1. The centre can be chain pieced easily by taking one half-square triangle unit pressed to the pink and sewing to one that is pressed to the light. Chain piece 36 units together. Cut thread and press open. Turn half round and sew 18 centre units (see diagram **i**), matching the centre seam. Press.

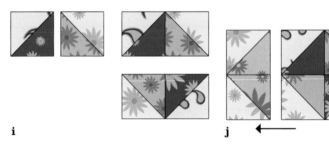

i   j

2. Sew a flying geese unit to either side of a centre unit (see diagram **j**). Press as shown by arrows.

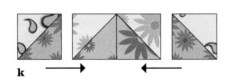

k

3. Sew a half-square triangle unit to either side of a flying geese unit as shown in diagram **k**. Make 36. Press as shown by arrows.

4. Assemble the blocks in rows as shown in diagram **l**. Your blocks can be as scrappy as you like. Press as shown.

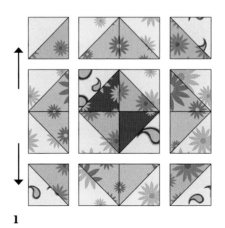

l

Sewing four patch units for star block two

1. Take one medium and one dark of the four patch strips and, with right sides together, sew down the long side (see diagram **m**). Open and press to darker side. Repeat with the other four patch strips.

2. Trim selvedge and cut 2½in segments from each strip unit (see diagram **n**). You need 34 in total.

3. Chain piece the 2½in segments together to form 17 four patch blocks. Cut threads and press four patch blocks open (see diagram **o**).

Sewing flying geese units for star block two

1. Take one red 2½in square and lay it right sides together on a 2½ x 4½in cream background rectangle. Sew across the diagonal as shown in diagram **p**.

2. Flip the square over to the top corner and press towards the red fabric (see diagram **q**). Trim the excess red fabric but do not trim the cream background fabric. Although this creates a little more bulk, this cream background rectangle keeps your flying geese in shape.

3. Place a second red 2½in square and lay it on the other side as shown and sew across the diagonal. Flip the square over and press towards the red fabric (see diagram **r**). Trim excess red fabric.

Assembling star block two

Assemble the blocks in rows as shown in diagram **s**, adding the squares you cut from the light strips. Your blocks can be as scrappy as you like or you might prefer to have the same flying geese units in one block. Play with the layout to decide the look you prefer. Press seams as shown.

m

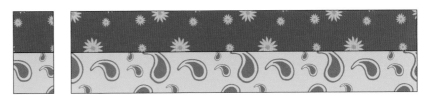

n

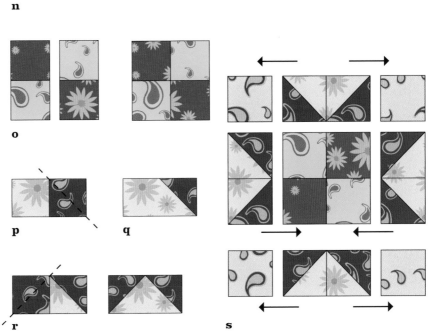

o

p   **q**

r   **s**

left:
This variation was made by Sue Morse who, after listening to an explanation of how the colour variations were quite important, went ahead and made it with a blue jelly roll! The result is stunning and proves how doing your own thing can produce great results.

t

Referring to diagram **t**, above, lay out the blocks into rows. Make seven rows of five blocks. When you are happy with the layout, sew the blocks into rows and then sew rows together. Pin at every seam intersection to ensure you have matching seams.

Finishing the quilt

Join your seven 2½in border strips into one continuous length and, referring to the instructions on page 122, add the borders to your quilt. Your quilt top is now complete. Quilt as desired and bind to finish.

|0 |½ |1 |1½ |2 |

Starlight Express

Vital statistics

Quilt size: 76 x 76in.
Block size: 29in.
Number of blocks: 4.
Setting: 2 x 2 blocks with 2in wide sashing and 6in wide border.

Can you believe it – there are no set-in seams or Y seams in this quilt! That should appeal to many who have avoided this stunning design in the past. This quilt goes together beautifully and will appeal to the more ambitious quilter. A beginner should start on one of the other projects and move on to this when they are confident about piecing diamonds with their bias edges.

We used a great range from Moda's Three Sisters against a neutral background. We did have to use 'artistic licence'

when dividing our jelly roll into different colours and our reds, out of necessity, ended up including creams and browns with just a hint of red! It did make us think that perhaps we do spend too much time searching for the exact colour we feel is necessary for a quilt. The pioneering women in their covered wagons heading West couldn't head off to the nearest quilt shop to find a specific colour and their antique quilts are hugely admired. There is a lesson to be learned there somewhere!

opposite:
Starlight Express is a project for the more experienced quilter as it involves piecing diamonds. The quilt was pieced by the authors and longarm quilted by The Quilt Room.

What you need

- One jelly roll or:
Four dark 2½in wide strips cut the width of the fabric.
Four light 2½in wide strips cut the width of the fabric.
Eight colour A (green) 2½in wide strips cut the width of the fabric.
12 colour B (red) 2½in wide strips cut the width of the fabric.
Eight colour C (blue) 2½in wide strips cut the width of the fabric.

- 3m (118in) border and background fabric.

- 60cm (23½in) binding fabric.

Cutting instructions

Jelly roll strips: Cut 10in from each of 36 strips and set aside for sashing. You will have four strips spare.

Background fabric:

• Cut four strips 9⅝in wide across the width of the fabric and sub-cut into 16 9⅝in squares. Cut in half diagonally to form 32 half-square triangles X.

• Cut three strips 7in wide across the width of the fabric and sub-cut into 16 7in squares. Cut in half diagonally to form 32 half-square triangles Y.

Borders: Cut eight 6½in wide strips across the width of the fabric.

Binding: Cut eight 2½in wide strips across the width of the fabric.

• Use a scant ¼in seam allowance throughout.

Sewing your strip units

There are three different rows in each diamond and you therefore need to make three different strip units as follows:

Strip unit A: Choose a dark, a green and a red strip and join in the order shown in diagram **a**, offsetting by 2in. It is important to offset the strips to avoid wasting fabric. Press seams to dark fabric. Make four strip unit As.

Strip unit B: Choose a green, a red and a blue strip and join in the order shown in diagram **b**, offsetting by 2in. Press seams to blue. Make four strip unit Bs.

Strip unit C: Choose a red, a blue and a light strip and join in the order shown in diagram **c**, offsetting by 2in. Press seams to red. Make four strip unit Cs.

a

b

c

Tip

Artistic licence may be used when sorting your strips and this will only enhance the individual look of the quilt (our reds included browns and creams with just a hint of red). If you prefer a more unified look, then you might have to swap a few strips with another jelly roll.

0   ½   1   1½   2

d

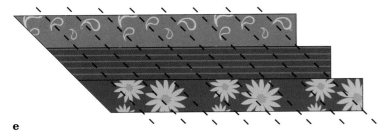

e

Cutting your strip units

1. Take one strip unit A and turn 180 degrees. Position your ruler over the uneven right edge aligning the 45 degree line on your ruler along the bottom edge of your strip unit. Trim as shown in diagram **d**. Turn back 180 degrees to start cutting your strips.

2. Line up your ruler along the angled cut and cut eight 2½in segments, as shown in diagram **e**. Keep these together as you will use the eight segments from the same strip unit A together with eight segments from a strip unit B and eight from a strip unit C to form one star.

Repeat until all your strip units are cut and put into separate piles. It can help to label them A, B or C as you cut each set of segments.

Tip

As you are cutting your strips, ensure the 45 degree line on your ruler is always running parallel to your seam lines. You do not want to deviate from cutting at a 45 degree angle. Every two or three strips, check that you are cutting accurately and trim your edge if necessary.

Sewing your diagrams

1. Choose one set each of strip units
A, B and C to form your first star (see
diagram **f**).

2. Take a unit A segment and sew it
to a unit B segment. To match the
seams, insert a pin through each seam
to secure before sewing (see diagram
g). You will notice that the rows will
appear ¼in out at each end but this is
because you have an angled cut. It is
important to check that your seams are
nicely matched before sewing.

3. Take a unit C segment and join to
complete one diamond. Trim all ears
to reduce bulk. Repeat until you have
eight diamonds. These will form your
first star (see diagram **h**).

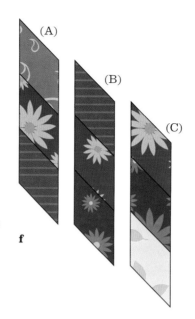

f

g

h

Completing the blocks

1. Sew a triangle X and a triangle Y (which you have cut from your background fabric) to either side of a diamond as shown in diagram **i**. They will both overlap ¼in each side of the diamond.

2. Repeat with another three diamonds. Repeat with the four other diamonds but this time placing triangle X and triangle Y on the opposite sides of the diamonds, as shown in diagram **j**.

3. Join the diamonds to form the star, carefully matching and pinning all seams before sewing. One star block is now complete. Repeat with your other strip units to form four star blocks in total.

above: *The variation called Retro Blossoms, using the funky fabric from Urban Chick with a pale green background, was pieced by Alison Wood of The Quilt Room. It was longarm quilted by The Quilt Room.*

i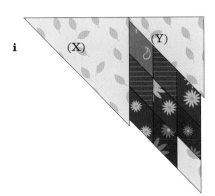

j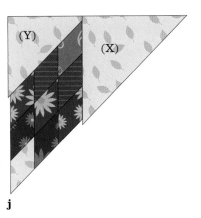

Adding your sashing

You have 36 10in strips set aside for the sashing plus four unused strips from the jelly roll if you wish to make any substitutes.

1. Take three 10in strips and join into a continuous length of 29in (you lose 1in in seam allowances). Your blocks measure 29in square so this is the correct length for your sashing. Repeat until you have 12 lengths of 29in.

2. From the balance of your fabric, cut nine 2½in squares for your sashing squares.

3. Join the sashing squares to the sashing as shown in diagram **k** and sew around the blocks, easing where necessary. Join all the blocks together.

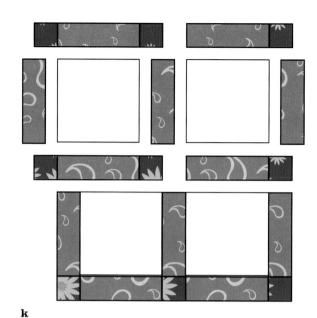

k

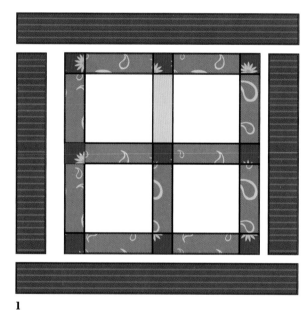

l

Finishing the quilt

Join your eight 6½in wide border strips into one continuous length and, referring to the instructions on page 122, add borders to the quilt (see diagram **l**). Your quilt top is now complete. Quilt as desired and bind to finish.

Both Sides of the Pond

Vital statistics

Quilt size: 72 x 72in.
Block size: 16in.
Number of blocks: 13 plus 2in wide border.

In addition to their love of quilting, one of the many things that American and British people have in common is the colour of their national flags – red, white and blue. So here is a patriotic quilt, whatever side of the 'pond' you live.

Now this quilt really needs some help from a friend as we took one red roll and one blue roll and used 18 reds and 21 blues. So all you need now is to find someone who would like to sew the same quilt but using the reds and blues the other way round – with 21 reds and 18 blues. What a great idea for a sociable quilting weekend!

What you need

- One jelly roll or 18 red 2½in wide strips cut across the width of the fabric.

- 21 blue 2½in wide strips cut across the width of the fabric.

- 3.75m (148in) light background fabric.

- 60cm (23½in) binding.

opposite:
Both Sides of the Pond uses four patch, nine patch and flying geese units to form a striking design. The quilt was pieced by the authors and longarm quilted by The Quilt Room.

Cutting instructions

Red strips: Take seven strips and cut into 2½in squares. You should get 16 to a strip. You need 104 squares. Leave the other red strips for making the nine patch blocks.

Blue strips: Take 12 strips and cut into 2½ x 4½in rectangles. You should get nine to a strip. You need 104.

Take seven strips and cut into 2½in squares. You should get 16 to a strip. You need 104 squares. Leave the other two blue strips for making the four patch blocks.

Background fabric:
• Cut 18 2½in wide strips across the width of the fabric. Set eight of these aside for the borders.
• Cut 11 4½in wide strips across the width of the fabric. Set seven aside for nine patch units.
• Sub-cut the remaining four strips into 2½in wide segments. You should get 16 to a strip. You need 52 2½ x 4½in rectangles.

• Cut two 24in strips. From each strip cut one 24in square and one 12½in square. These are for the setting and corner triangles.
• Cut across both diagonals of each of the 24in squares to form eight setting triangles. Cut across one diagonal of each of the 12½in squares to form four corner triangles (see diagram **a**).

Cutting the setting and corner triangles this way ensures the outer edges of your quilt are not on the bias.

Binding: Cut eight 2½in wide strips across the width of the fabric.

• Use a scant ¼in seam allowance throughout.

24"   12½"

a

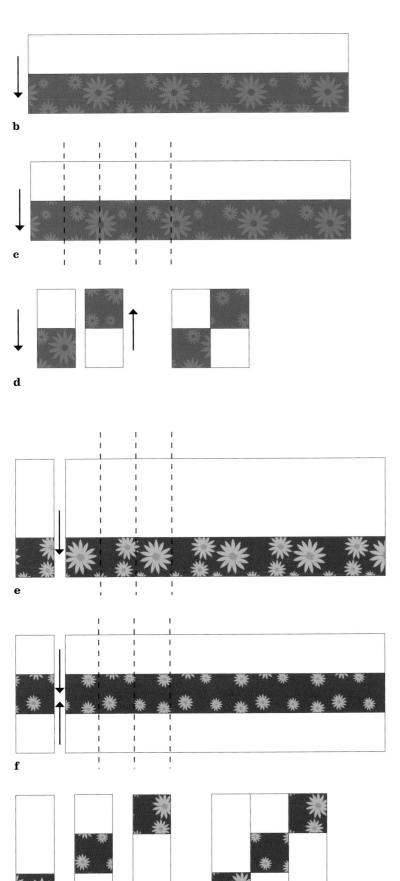

b

c

d

e

f

g

Sewing the four patch blocks

1. Take a 2½in wide light strip (from the background fabric) and a 2½in wide blue strip and sew together (see diagram **b**). Repeat with another 2½in wide light strip and a 2½in wide blue strip. Press to dark side.

2. Cut both joined strips into 2½in segments as shown in diagram **c**. You need 26 segments.

3. Match the centre seams and sew your four patch (see diagram **d**). You need 13. Press to dark fabric.

Tip

For accuracy, don't stackpile your strips when cutting the segments for the four patch blocks. Check you are cutting perfect rectangles by putting one of your ruler guides on the seam line.

Sewing the nine patch blocks

1. Take a 4½in light strip and sew it to a 2½in red strip. Press to the dark side. Repeat until you have seven units. Cut each unit into 2½in segments (see diagram **e**). You should get 16 to a unit. You need 104.

2. Take a 2½in light strip and sew it to a 2½in red strip. Press to the red. Take another 2½in white strip and sew it to the other side of the red. Repeat until you have four units. Cut each unit into 2½in segments (see diagram **f**). You should get 16 to a unit. You need 52.

3. Assemble the nine patch blocks as shown in diagram **g**, making sure that the seams are neatly aligned. Press. You need 52 nine patch blocks.

Sewing the flying geese units

1. Take one blue 2½in square and lay it right sides together on a 2½ x 4½in light rectangle. Sew across the diagonal as shown in diagram **h**. Draw the diagonal line in first to mark your stitching line if it helps.

2. Flip the square over and press towards the blue fabric (see diagram **i**). Trim the excess blue fabric but do not trim the light fabric. Although this creates a little more bulk, this light rectangle will keep your flying geese in shape.

3. Place a second blue 2½in square on the other side of the rectangle as shown in diagram **j** and sew across the diagonal. Flip the square over and press.

4. Trim excess blue fabric. Repeat until you have 52 of these units (diagram **k**).

5. Following the instructions above, take 52 of the blue rectangles and 104 red squares and make 52 units shown in diagram **l**.

6. Sew one flying geese unit to either side of a blue rectangle making sure you place them as shown in diagram **m**. Press both flying geese units to blue rectangle. You need 52 of these units.

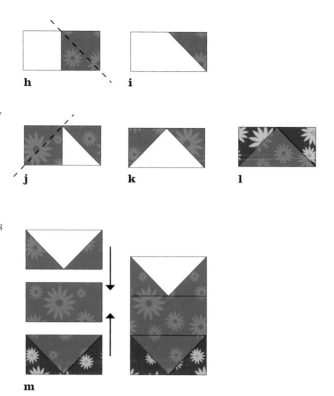

h   i

j   k   l

m

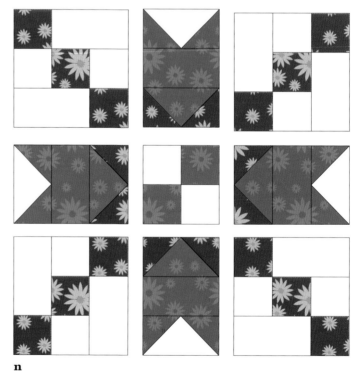

n

Assembling the blocks

Join the units into rows rotating the units as shown in diagram **n**. Join the rows together to form the block. You need to make 13 of these blocks.

above:
This variation, called Green Beans, and Red Berries, was pieced by Gwen Jones of The Quilt Room in a festive green and red with a cream background and longarm quilted by The Quilt Room.

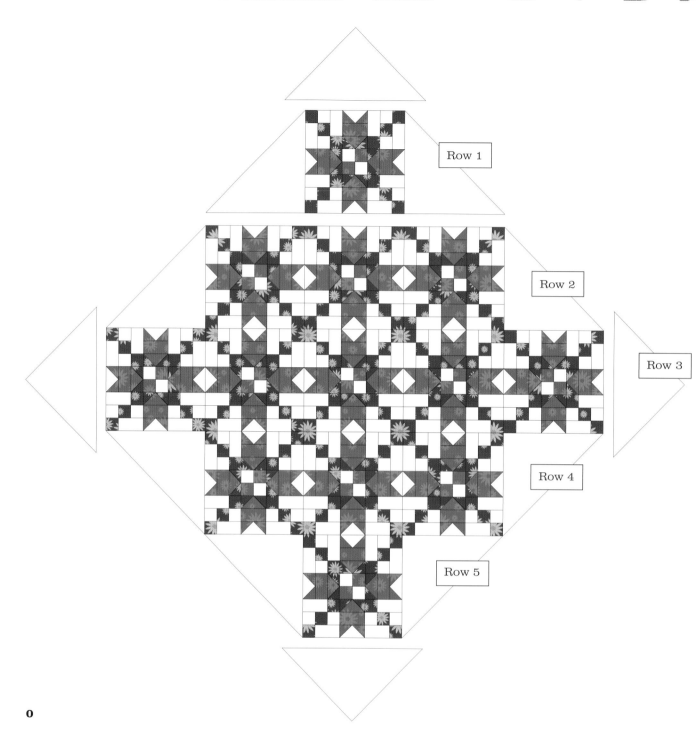

Row 1

Row 2

Row 3

Row 4

Row 5

o

Setting blocks on point

Referring to diagram **o,** sew a setting
triangle to each side of a block to create
row 1. Continue to sew the blocks
together as shown in the diagram to
form rows with a setting triangle at
each end. Sew the corner triangles on
last. Trim edges to square up quilt.

Finishing the quilt

Join your eight 2½in wide border
strips into one continuous length
and, referring to the instructions
on page 122, add borders to
the quilt. Your quilt top is now
complete. Quilt as desired and
bind to finish.

0   ½   1   1½   2

Quilt Carry Bag

Vital statistics

Size: 33in wide, stretching over 45in when full of quilts.

This bag is deceptively spacious and holds more quilts than you would imagine. If you are off to a 'show and tell', it is perfect for transporting everything safely. It is stitched using the stitch and flip method, which makes up really quickly.

What you need

• 26 strips from a jelly roll, or 2½in wide strips, cut across the width of varied fabrics.

• 130 x 82½cm (52 x 33in) natural calico.

• 130 x 82½cm (52 x 33in) thin wadding.

• Two lengths of cord each approx. 150cm (60in) long.

• Six magnetic poppers.

above left and opposite:
This large carry bag is just what you need to store or transport your quilts. It was made by Tina Lamborn of The Quilt Room.

Tip

It is important that all quilts, however small, are signed and dated either on the front, making a feature of it, or on the back. Also, why not put some interesting details about the quilt – why it was made, who it was made for and how long it took? We all know how interested we are when finding details like this about old quilts – let's give the quilters of the future an easier time in their research.

Cutting the strips

Cut a 35in length from each strip. Save the excess for making the bag handles.

Instructions

1. Place the wadding on to the calico and baste around the edge to secure (see diagram **a**).

2. Place one strip right side up on one edge with a second strip wrong side up directly on top of it, overlapping the wadding 1in at the top and bottom (see diagram **b**). You need this amount each end without the wadding underneath it to create the hem for the cord without having too much bulk. Using a ¼in seam allowance, sew down the strip as shown.

3. Open the second strip out and finger press. Sew a third strip down in the same way. Continue across until your wadding and calico are covered (see diagram **c**).

4. At both short ends, turn under a hem of 1½in and stitch down securely. These are the two ends where the poppers will go.

5. On both long sides, turn under a hem of at least ½in and stitch down securely. These are to thread the cord through.

6. Using the excess from the strips, join together to make two strips approximately 112in long for handles. Lay the two strips right sides together and sew down both long sides and one short side. Turn right sides out and press.

a

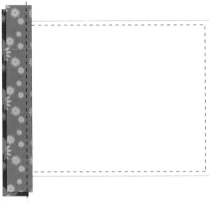

b

c

|0 |½ |1 |1½ |2|

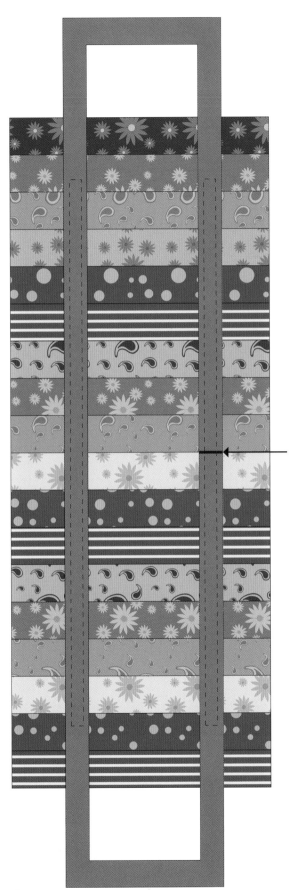

7. Lay out the bag and place the handle strip on top, 6in in from the edge of the long side and marking the points where the stitching has to stop at each corner. This should be approximately 9½in from the short side. Make sure you have the same amount of handle at each end left unstitched.

8. Start sewing where shown by the arrow in diagram **d** to ensure that the join of the handle goes underneath the bag. Stitch securely in place.

9. Thread the lengths of cord through the long ends of the bag and make a large knot at each end. We then used some fabric to fashion a covering for the knot but you could use a toggle or be as creative as you like.

10. Sew the magnetic poppers to the short ends of the bag spacing them out evenly. Fill the bag with quilts and off you go!

d

Tip

Change your sewing machine needles frequently. Dull or bent needles can snag and distort your fabric and cause your machine to skip stitches. Make sure the tension is adjusted properly so you are producing smooth, even seams.

General Techniques

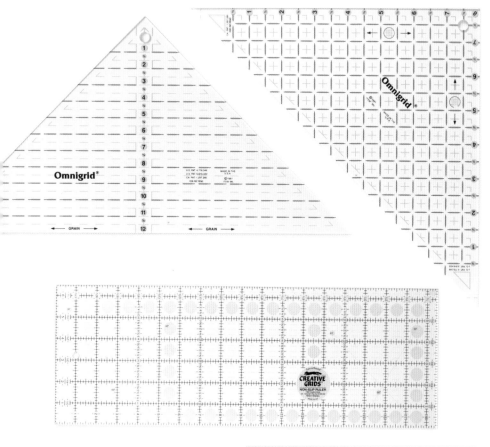

Tools

All the projects in this book require rotary cutting equipment. You will need a self-healing cutting mat at least 18 x 24in and a rotary cutter. We recommend the 45mm or the 60mm rotary cutter.

Any rotary cutting work requires rulers and most people have a make they prefer. We like the Creative Grids rulers as their markings are clear, they do not slip on the fabric and their Turn-A-Round facility is so useful when dealing with half-inch measurements. We recommend the 6½ x 24½in as a basic ruler plus a large square no less than 12½in, which is handy for squaring up and making sure you are always cutting at right angles.

We have tried not to use too many different speciality rulers but when working with 2½in strips you do have to rethink some cutting procedures. The Omnigrid 96 or the larger 96L, is widely available from quilting suppliers. It is used for cutting half-square triangles as in *Twin Stars* and also for cutting trapezoids as in *Friendship Braid*. The Omnigrid 98L is for cutting quarter-square triangles. We use it in our quilt *Garden Trellis*. If you are using any other tool, please make sure you are lining up your work on the correct markings.

top left: **Omnigrid 98L.**
top right: **Omnigrid 96L.**
centre: **Creative Grid 6½ x 24½in rectangle.**
right: **Creative Grid 8½ in square.**

Seams

We cannot stress enough the importance of maintaining an accurate ¼in seam allowance throughout. We prefer to say an accurate scant ¼in seam because there are two factors to take into consideration. Firstly, the thickness of thread and secondly, when you press your seam allowance to one side it takes up a tiny amount of fabric, which has to be allowed for. These are both extremely small amounts but if they are ignored you will find your exact ¼in seam allowance is taking up more than ¼in.

It is well worth testing your seam allowance before starting on a quilt and most sewing machines have various needle positions that can be used to make any adjustments.

Pressing

In quiltmaking, pressing is of vital importance and if extra care is taken you will be well rewarded. This is especially true when dealing with strips. If your strips start bowing and stretching you will lose accuracy.

• Always set your seam after sewing by pressing the seam as sewn, without opening up your strips (see diagram **a**). This eases any tension and prevents the seam line from distorting.

Move the iron with an up and down motion, zig-zagging along the seam rather than ironing down the length of the seam which could cause distortion.

• Open up your strips and press on the right side of the fabric towards the darker fabric, if necessary guiding the seam underneath to make sure the seam is going in the right direction (see diagram **b**). Press with an up and down motion rather than along the length of the strip.

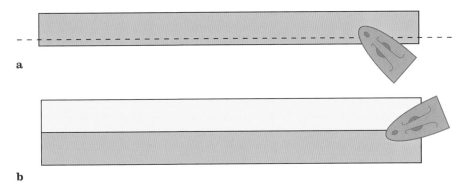

a

b

Seam allowance test

Take a 2½in strip and cut off three segments 1½in wide. Sew two segments together down the longer side and press seam to one side. Sew the third segment across the top. It should fit exactly. If it doesn't, you need to make an adjustment to your seam allowance. If it is too long, your seam allowance is too wide and can be corrected by moving the needle on your sewing machine to the right. If it is too small, your seam allowance is too narrow and this can be corrected by moving the needle to the left.

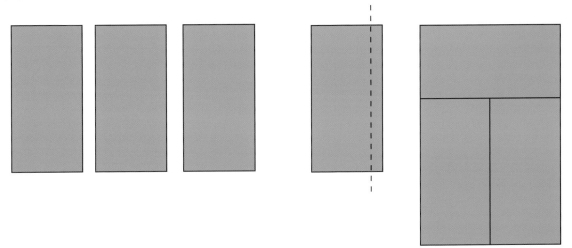

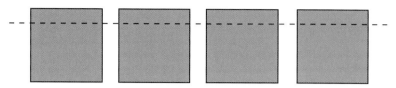

• Always take care if using steam and certainly don't use steam anywhere near a bias edge.

• When you are joining more than two strips together, press the seams after attaching each strip. You are far more likely to get bowing if you leave it until your strip unit is complete before pressing.

• Each seam must be pressed flat before another seam is sewn across it. Unless there is a special reason for not doing so, seams are pressed towards the darker fabric. The main criteria when joining seams, however, is to have the seam allowances going in the opposite direction to each other as they then nest together without bulk. Your patchwork will lie flat and your seam intersections will be accurate.

Pinning

Don't underestimate the benefits of pinning. When you have to align a seam it is important to insert pins to stop any movement when sewing. Long, fine pins with flat heads are recommended as they will go through the layers of fabric easily and allow you to sew up to and over them.

Seams should always be pressed in opposite directions so they will nest together nicely. Insert a pin either at right angles or diagonally through the seam intersection ensuring that the seams are matching perfectly. When sewing, do not remove the pin too early as your fabric might shift and your seams will not be perfectly aligned.

c

Chain piecing

Chain-piecing is the technique of feeding a series of pieces through the sewing machine without lifting the presser foot and without cutting the thread between each piece (see diagram **c** above). Always chain piece when you can – it saves time and thread. Once your chain is complete, simply snip the thread between the pieces.

When chain piecing shapes other than squares and rectangles, it is sometimes preferable, when finishing one shape, to lift the presser foot slightly and reposition on the next shape, still leaving the thread uncut.

Instructions for adding borders

The fabric requirements in this book all assume you are going to be sewing straight rather than mitred borders. If you intend to have mitred borders please add sufficient fabric for this.

1. Begin by sewing all your border strips into one continuous length. These strips may be straight from the jelly roll or cut from separate fabric, according to the instructions given for each quilt.

2. Determine the vertical measurement from top to bottom through the centre of your quilt top (see diagram **d**). Cut two side border strips to this measurement. Mark the halves and quarters of one quilt side and one border with pins. Placing right sides together and matching the pins, stitch quilt and border together, easing the quilt side to fit where necessary. Repeat on the opposite side.

3. Determine the horizontal measurement from side to side across the centre of the quilt top. Cut two top and bottom border strips to this measurement and add to the quilt top in the same manner (see diagram **e**).

d

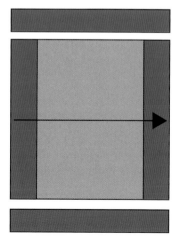

e

Dog ears to go

A dog ear is the excess piece of fabric which overlaps past the seam allowance when sewing triangles to other shapes. Dog ears should always be cut off to reduce bulk. They can be trimmed using a rotary cutter although snipping with small sharp scissors is quicker. Make sure you are trimming the points parallel to the straight edge of the triangle

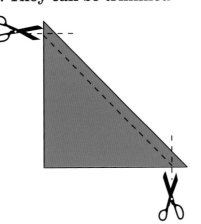

Quilting

Quilting stitches hold the patchwork top, wadding and backing together and create texture over your finished patchwork. The choice is yours whether you hand quilt, machine quilt or send it off to a longarm quilting service. There are many books dedicated to the techniques of hand and machine quilting but the basic procedure is as follows:

1. With the aid of templates or a ruler, mark out the quilting lines on the patchwork top.

2. Cut the backing and wadding at least 3in larger all around than the patchwork top. Pin or tack the layers together to prepare them for quilting.

3. Quilt either by hand or by machine.

below: **Pineapple Surprise** *detail showing a rose meander quilting design, which compliments the geometric patchwork.*

Stop ¼in from the end

a

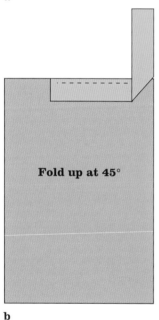

Fold up at 45°

b

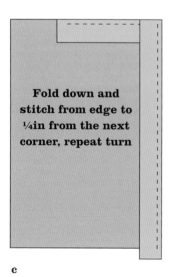

Fold down and stitch from edge to ¼in from the next corner, repeat turn

c

Instructions for binding your quilt

The fabric requirements in this book are for a 2½in double-fold French binding cut on the straight of grain.

• Trim the excess backing and wadding so that the edges are even with the top of the quilt.

• Join your binding strips into a continuous length, making sure there is sufficient to go around the quilt plus 8-10in for the corners and overlapping ends.

• With wrong sides together, press the binding in half lengthways. Fold and press under ½in to neaten the edge at the end where you will start sewing.

• On the right side of the quilt and starting around 12in away from a corner, align the edges of the double thickness binding with the edge of the quilt so that the cut edges are towards the edges of the quilt and pin to hold in place. Sew with a ¼in seam allowance, leaving the first inch open.

• At the first corner, stop ¼in from the edge of the fabric and backstitch (see diagram **a**). Lift needle and presser foot and fold as shown in diagram **b**, then fold again as shown in diagram **c**. Stitch from the edge to ¼in from next corner and repeat the turn.

• Continue all around the quilt working each corner in the same way. When you come to the starting point, cut the binding, fold under the cut edge and overlap at the starting point.

• Fold over the binding to the back of the quilt and hand stitch in place. At each corner, fold the binding to form a neat mitre.

How to calculate for a larger quilt

In this book we have shown what can be achieved with one jelly roll. We have sometimes added background fabric and borders but the basis of each featured quilt is just one roll.

If you want to make a larger version of any quilt, refer to the Vital Statistics of the quilt, which shows the block size, the number of blocks, how the blocks are set plus the size of border used.

Example: You would like to make a quilt 92 x 108in for a double bed using the *Pandora's Box* pattern.

• Referring to the Vital Statistics, our quilt is 52 x 76in and you can see that we made 40 8in blocks plus we added a 6in border. If you want your quilt to measure 92 x 108in, firstly deduct the 6in borders from all sides. This leaves a size of 80 x 96in. You now know you need sufficient blocks to make a size 80 x 96in. As the block size is 8in you need 10 x 12 blocks = 120 blocks.

• We used one jelly roll to make 40 blocks so you need three jelly rolls to make 120 blocks. You just have to buy additional jelly rolls!

Tips for setting on point

Floral Bouquet and *Both Sides of the Pond* are both examples of quilts set diagonally or 'on point'. The patterns contain all the information you need to make the quilts. However, any block can take on a totally new look when set on point and you might like to try one of the other quilts to see what it looks like on point. Some people are a little daunted by the prospect, but here is all you need to know.

• To calculate the measurement of the block from point to point you multiply the size of the finished block by 1.414.
Example: A 12in block will measure 12in x 1.414, which is 16.97in (just under 17in).

• Piece rows diagonally, starting at a corner. Triangles have to be added to the end of each row before joining the rows and these are called setting triangles.

• Setting triangles form the outside of your quilt and need to have the straight of grain on the outside edge to prevent stretching. To ensure this, these triangles are formed from quarter square triangles, i.e. a square cut into four. To calculate the size of the square, use this formula:
Diagonal block size + 1¼in
Example: A 12in block (diagonal measurement approx. 17in) would need to be 18¼in.

• Corner triangles are added last. They also need to have the outside edge on the straight of grain so these should be cut from half-square triangles. To calculate the size of square to cut in half, divide the finished size of your block by 1.414 then add ⅞in.
Example: A 12in block would be 12in divided by 1.414 = 8.49in + ⅞in (0.88) = 9.37in (or 9½in as it can be trimmed later).

above: *The simple square takes on a totally different look when set on point and transformed into a diamond.*

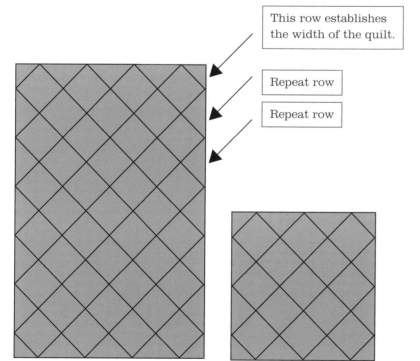

This row establishes the width of the quilt.

Repeat row

Repeat row

d

The type of diagonal quilt we have used in this book starts off with one block and in each row thereafter the number of blocks increases by two. All rows contain an odd number of blocks. To figure the finished size of the quilt, you count the number of diagonals across and multiply this by the diagonal measurement of the block. Do the same with the number of blocks down and multiply this by the diagonal measurement of the block.

If you want a rectangular quilt instead of a square one, you count the number of blocks in the row that establishes the width (see diagram **d**) and repeat that number in following rows until you have reached the desired length.

Fabric requirements when not using a jelly roll

You might wish to make a less 'scrappy' quilt and would like to substitute larger amounts of the same fabrics rather than use jelly rolls. Perhaps you have a bundle of ten fabrics you want to use or maybe you only want to use two. The following table will enable you to calculate how much you require of each fabric, however many fabrics you intend to use in your quilt.

Number of fabrics to be used instead of a jelly roll	Amount required of each fabric
2 fabrics (20 strips of each)	1.4m (55in)
3 fabrics (14 strips of each)	1m (39½in)
4 fabrics (10 strips of each)	1.1m (43¼in)
5 fabrics (8 strips of each)	60cm (23½in)
6 fabrics (7 strips of each)	50cm (20in)
7 fabrics (6 strips of each)	50cm (20in)
8 or 9 fabrics (5 strips of each)	40cm (16in)
10-13 fabrics (4 strips of each)	30cm (12in)
14-19 fabrics (3 strips of each)	25cm (10in)

Note: If you are using fat quarters, these are only half the width of the fabric so you must double the number of strips to be used. You can get seven strips from both a fat quarter yard and a fat quarter metre – you might even be able to squeeze eight strips from a fat quarter metre.

Acknowledgments

Pam and Nicky would firstly like to thank Susan Rogers at Moda Fabrics for introducing them to jelly rolls and for insisting they 'just try some'. They would also like to thank Mark Dunn of Moda for allowing them to entitle the book Jelly Roll Quilts.

They would also like to thank the girls in both the shop and the warehouse for their help and encouragement at every turn with special thanks to Alison, Gwen and Tina for making up some of the variations and to Sharon and Margaret for being such excellent 'strippers' at our Quilt Room Strip Club! Many thanks also to Isabelle and Kath at Southill Piecemakers for coming to our aid.

Their thanks also to Paul and Mildred Statler who travelled to England to teach them all they needed to know about the Statler Stitcher. Without their initial help they would never have learned everything so quickly to make the deadlines for this book.

Last but not least, special thanks to Pam's husband Nick for his continued support over the last 27 quilting years since The Quilt Room has been open and to Nicky's partner Rob and his daughter Natalie who, although haven't quite had 27 quilting years' experience, are fast becoming experts with terms such as fat quarters and strip clubs!

above, l to r:
Pam and Nicky Lintott

About the authors

Pam opened The Quilt Room in 1981, which she still runs today along with her daughter, Nicky. She is the author of *The Quilt Room, Patchwork & Quilting Workshops*, as well as *The Quilter's Workbook*.

Nicky began working at The Quilt Room three years ago and is now in charge of producing their mail order catalogue and running their internet site. She also has taken on the long arm quilting side of the business which is taking up more and more of her time. All the quilts in this book were long arm quilted by her.

Useful Contacts

The Quilt Room
20 West Street
Dorking, Surrey
England, RH4 1BL
tel: 01306 740739
www.quiltroom.co.uk
Mail order department:
Rear of Carvilles, Station Road
Dorking, Surrey, England
RH4 1XH
tel: 01306 877307

Moda Fabrics/United Notions
13800 Hutton Drive
Dallas, TX 75234, USA
tel: (800) 527-9447
www.modafabrics.com

Creative Grids (UK) Ltd
Unit 1J, Peckleton Lane
Business Park
Peckleton Lane, Peckleton
Leicester, Leics
England, LE9 7RN
tel: 01455 828667
www.creativegrids.com

Lecien Fabric
European Distributor:
Rhinetex B V
Geurdeland 7
6673 Dr Andelst
Netherlands
tel: (31) 488 480030
www.rhinetex.com
US Distributor:
The Gary L Marcus Co Inc
11 Brownwood Lane
Norwich, CT 06360, USA

tel: (860) 887 6614
email: glmarcusco@aol.com
For other countries visit
www.lecien.co.jp

**Daiwabo Co Ltd
(Japanese Taupes)**
For shops and distributor
information visit
www.pinwheelstrading.com

**Kaffe Fassett & Heather
Bailey Fabric**
European Distributor:
Rowan Yarns
Green Lane Mill,
Holmfirth, England
HD9 2DX
tel: 01484 681881
US Distributor:
Westminster Fibers Inc
165 Ledge Street
NH 03060, USA
tel: (800) 445 9276

Anna Griffin Fabric
European Distributor:
Anbo Textiles Ltd
Unit 8-9 Dashwood Industrial
Estate, Dashwood Avenue
High Wycombe, Bucks.
England, HP12 3ED
tel: 01494 450155
email: otto@anbo.co.uk
US Distributor:
Windham Fabrics/Baum Textiles
Baum Textile Mills, Inc
812 Jersey Avenue
Jersey City, NJ 07310, USA

tel: (201) 659 0444
www.windhamfabrics.com

**Fossil Fern Fabrics – US
Benartex Inc.**
1359 Broadway, Suite 1100
New York, NY 10018
tel: (212) 840 3250
www.benartex.com
European Distributor:
Ebor Fabrics Ltd.
Embsay Mills
Embsay, Skipton
N Yorks, England, BD23 6QF
tel: 01756 793908

**Thirties & Reproduction Fabrics by
Judie Rothermel**
Marcus Brothers.
www.marcusbrothers.com or
Anbo Textiles (European Distributor)

**Reproduction Fabrics by Jo Morton
Andover Fabrics**
www.andoverfabrics.com
Makower UK Ltd
118 Greys Road,
Henley-on-Thames, Oxon
England, RG9 1QW
tel: 01491 579727
www.makoweruk.com

Index

Entries in italics indicate a quilt name

allowance, seam 9, 16, 86, 121
Anna Griffin fabrics 78
April Cornell fabrics 61, 67

backing 123
Bars of Gold 10-13
bias edges 57, 122
binding 124
Blackbird Designs 24
blocks, four patch 17
Blue Lagoon 14-19
borders, adding 122
    mitred 122
Both Sides of the Pond 108-15, 125
bowing, preventing 12
braids 81-2

calculating fabrics 126
    sizes 124
chain piecing 12, 48, 122
Chinese Coins 10
Civil War Scrappy 36-9
corner triangles 125
Creative Grid ruler 120
cutting mat 120

Daisy Chain 62-9
diagonal quilt patterns 124
diamond piecing 100, 104
dog ears 123
dragonfly quilting 40

easing fabric 13

Fig Tree Quilt fabrics 54
Floral Bouquet 70-77, 125
flying geese units 96-7, 108, 112
Fossils in the Garden 70, 76
four patch blocks 14, 16-17, 42, 97,
    108, 111
French binding 124
Fresh 17
Friendship Braid 78-83

Garden Trellis 24-9
Green Beans and Red Berries 113

half-square triangles 92, 94-5,
    125
hand quilting 123
hanging quilts 33
Heather Bailey fabrics 62
hourglass block 30-3

Inky's Quilt 81
ironing 121-22
It's Not a Gold Watch! 27

Japanese taupe fabrics 40, 81
Jo Morton fabrics 36
joining binding strips 122, 124
Judie Rothermel fabrics 36, 43

Kaffe Fasset fabrics 10, 20

Lecien Antique Fabrics 30
log cabin blocks 48-9
Log Cabin Hidden Stars 46-53
longarm quilting 123

machine quilting 123
machine sewing 74
    needles 119
    tension 74, 119
measurements 9
Moda fabrics 7, 8, 51, 100

nine patch blocks 30-2, 36, 38,
    108, 111
Nine Patch Wonder 30-35

Omnigrid 26-7, 80-81, 92, 94, 120
on point quilts 125

Pandora's Box 40-45, 124
Pineapple Surprise 84-91, 123
pinning 122
Plum Pie 61
pressing 12, 95, 121-2

quarter squares 56, 58, 125
Quilt Carry Bag 116-19
Quilt from Aunt Grace, A 43
quilting patterns
    dragonfly 40
    rose meander 123

Retro Blossoms 105
rose meander quilting 123
rotary cutter 87, 120
rotary cutting square 27
rulers 120

Sandy Gervaise fabrics 70
seams 9, 16, 86, 121-2
setting on point 125
setting triangles 125
snowball blocks 36, 38-9
Sparkling Gemstone 20-23
Spiral Strips 54-61
Stacked Coins 10
star block 96-7, 104
Starlight Express 100-107
stitch and flip 116
strip units 12, 56, 64-5, 102-3

triangles 125
templates 80, 94, 123
Terry Clothier Thompson fabrics
    46
Twin Stars 92-9

Urban Chick fabrics 105
Utopia 51

wadding 123
washing instructions 9